LOOKING AT MUSIC   Edited by Lina Brion and Detlef Diederichsen, with contributions by Stefanie Alisch, Peter Kirn, Mari Matsutoya, Adam Parkinson, Terre Thaemlitz, and TOPLAP

Looking at Music

Edited by
Lina Brion and Detlef Diederichsen

Contents

Looking at Music

"You have to accept that people hear music with their eyes first," saxophonist Branford Marsalis told *JazzTimes* magazine in 2019. "That's why the operative verb is 'see' when you go to a concert, not 'hear.'"[1] But what if there's nothing left to see at a concert—at least nothing exciting? Traditionally, a concert allows you to watch music being created, providing a much more intimate and intense musical experience than simply listening to it. As a result of digitalization, however, music has escaped the creative power of players and musical instruments, finding its way into existence by other means.

The performance of computer-produced music thus breaks with the centuries-old codes of the concert. To follow the usually quite laborious creation of these pieces in real time would be neither easy to organize nor very entertaining. A subsequent performance with such pre-produced sounds lacks the decisive element of a conventional concert—its "liveness." The laptop performance has now established a format in which the audience stares at people staring at screens. After decades the joke persists that, you have no idea whether the performers aren't just checking their e-mails or doing their tax returns. The musical instrument—computer software—is immaterial and thus invisible. Yet, above all, such a concert experience lacks the observable connection between gesture and sound. Just as the invention of the phonogram at the end of the nineteenth century entailed an initial uncoupling of the auditory from the visual experience, this mode also constitutes a historical break. Computer musician and engineer W. Andrew Schloss intimated this almost twenty years ago: The use of computers in live performances has, for the first time in the history of music-making obfuscated the relationship between cause and effect.[2] For thousands of years music was played with acoustic instruments, and, according to Schloss, it was always obvious which gesture produced which sound (blowing, bowing, plucking, beating); the audience could understand what was happening on stage. Computer-generated music suspends this physical law; from

---

1 Cited in *Wire*, no. 441 (2020), p. 14.
2 See W. Andrew Schloss, "Using Contemporary Technology in Live Performance: The Dilemma of the Performer," *Journal of New Music Research*, vol. 31, no. 1 (2002), pp. 239-42.

the audience's point of view, the relationship between musician and instrument seems "like magic," and there is no discernible proof that the audible sounds actually are produced "live."

Other approaches exist: Some artists dispense with the stage-centered spectacle altogether, instead emphasizing the collective listening experience. Others focus on the virtuoso staging of dance performances and playback sounds rather than on musical craftsmanship. Neither approach is concerned with the authenticity of the live experience. At the same time, the difficult conditions for performing programmed music have led to a number of technological innovations in recent years: from the screen views of live coders at algoraves to sensor-based digital musical instruments and virtual reality shows, visual stimuli and spontaneous artistic decisions are being reintroduced into electronic music performances on a variety of levels.

What role does visibility play in the experience of music? How important is the live character for the future of music performance? *Looking at Music* explores the question of whether music performance is in a state of crisis or whether new production possibilities, in fact, generate new types of performance.

The emergence of electronic music was accompanied early on by the departure from established live music principles. At "concerts," musicians would often sit among the audience with tape recorders and mixers, playing their tracks while everyone sat facing the speaker rig on stage, experiencing the music as an auditory narrative.[3] However, as electronic music moved beyond this mostly academic context, gaining greater popularity and becoming incorporated into established concert formats, the choice of performance format also became an economic question.

In this volume, the 1997 text by Terre Thaemlitz ponders the implications of this development for experimental music scenes such as computer-based ambient and, referencing Jacques Attali, criticizes the "implications of performance as a strategy of representation within the mechanisms of consumer capitalism." Contemporary digital music experimentalists, by contrast, are once again increasingly

---

3   See Kim Cascone, "Grain, Sequence, System: Three Levels of Reception in the Performance of Laptop Music," *Intelligent Agent*, vol. 4, no. 1 (2004), pp. 101–4.

committed to the legibility of music creation, in a literal sense: in the live coding scene, the computer screen is projected behind the performers, while the sound is created with typed code. The TOPLAP Manifesto has laid down the basic rules for this. *Looking at Music* heeds its demand to "Show us your screens," mapping screenshots from music productions of the last twenty years. Peter Kirn talks to musician and sound design lecturer Adam Parkinson about the role of the computer as an instrument, the use of algorithms to produce music, and the meaning of gestures and movements in laptop performances. Mari Matsutoya explains the great popularity and cultural origins of hologram performances and artificial vocals in Japan, using the example of the "virtual idol" Hatsune Miku. Stefanie Alisch looks at music seen as movement: Starting from the sophisticated dance vocabulary of the kuduro music scene (where a new track is usually released with a new dance step) to the kinetic music knowledge inherent in air guitar playing and air DJing, she explains "that any connection between sound and body movement perceived as natural is ultimately produced through performance."

In any case, the options and codes of music performance are, and remain, diverse, regardless of whether you hear it with your eyes, see it with your ears, or feel it through the imitation of movement.

Lina Brion and Detlef Diederichsen

Translated from the German by Kevin Kennedy

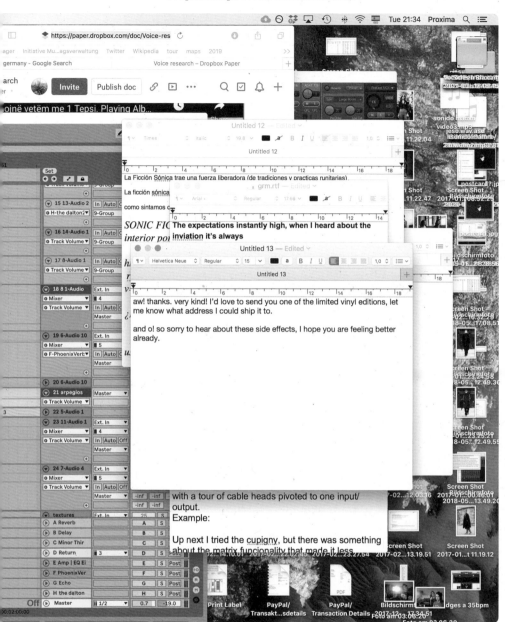

The Crisis of Post-Spectacle "Live" Contemporary Ambient Performance

(Or.. Why I Can't Get Paid to DJ A-Structural Audio)[1]

It is largely assumed among producers and listeners that the performance of contemporary ambient music incorporates a strategic con-
volution of noise with composition, presenting listeners with experiential conditions that emphasize their own performance within a
sonically active social theater, rather than suppressing their performance in favor of frontal spectacle. Similarly, it is well known that
production methods for contemporary ambient music, such as non-
real-time computer synthesis, typically involve processes which are
not immediately reconcilable with conventional listener/virtuoso
performance paradigms. However, when it comes to "live" contemporary ambient performance, there seems to be a great deal of
regressive desire among producers, organizers, and audiences for
conventional stage-based performance. This differentiation between
concepts of production and performance encompasses what Jacques
Attali referred to as economies of repetition and representation.

According to this model, processes of musical production and
distribution engage an economy of repetitions in which "[the producer's] income is independent of the quantity of labor he provides.
Instead, it depends on the quantity of demand for that labor. He pro-
duces the mold from which an industry is built."[2] Performance, on the
other hand, partakes in an economy of representation in which the
direct labor of the producer results in value for exchange: the show. Of
course, missing from Attali's analysis is the manner in which these
economies are inextricably intertwined, as record sales impact performance draw (including an impact upon a DJ's selection of materi-
als to play), and vice versa. However, if we concede Attali's assertion

---

1   This text was originally produced in April 1997 for a collection of essays
    by Mille Plateaux, but the book project was ultimately cancelled. It was
    first published in 2006 in a bilingual edition (English and Italian) by Nero
    Books.
2   Jacques Attali, *Noise: The Political Economy of Music*. Minneapolis, MN:
    University of Minnesota Press, 1985, p. 40.

that "in music, as in the rest of economy, the logic of the succession of musical codes parallels the logic of the creation of value,"[3] then perhaps the failings and contradictions of an economy around contemporary ambient performance may be expressed in terms of an unconscious attempt to reconcile antithetical musical codes of repetition and representation, rather than a deliberate exploitation of their multiplicity—a multiplicity which is suggested by ambient music's historical claim to address a restructuring and multiplication of cultural relations between production, performance, and listening.

Integral to any concept of performance is a strategic understanding of the means of production to be performed. For producers such as myself, who are almost entirely dependent upon computer synthesis, there is little room (and even less necessity) for the real-time modulation of elements during final mixing.[4] The heroics of authorial gesture are replaced by the uneventful establishment of variable programming parameters. Spontaneity and decisiveness occur throughout the compositional process, but unlike in modernist compositional strategies, they are not cherished as golden nuggets of primal and universal humanist contents.

The ultimate inclusion or exclusion of serendipity is understood in terms of editorial decision-making rather than divine manifestation, subjecting such occurrences to the same processes of social

3   Ibid., p. 41.
4   While several companies and educational institutions are developing "accessible" real-time synthesis software packages on several computer platforms, the majority of products remain expensive and not user friendly. This tends to limit their utilization to persons associated with production houses or educational institutions that can provide the financial backing required to immerse oneself in such processes. Even when real-time synthesis is implemented in a rather user-friendly manner—such as Arboretum Systems' GUI-friendly standalone application Hyperprism for the Power Mac—the real-time thruput can only apply to one sound at a time and, on slower machines, presents a significant increase in errors (heard as pops) compared to using the same program to process effects to a new sound file (a non-real time process). Multifile real-time processing through plug-ins, such as TDM and VST, still relies upon costly secondary processor systems, Pro Tools for example, or the speed of high-end CPUs. Thus, non-real-time sound generation remains the primary form of computer synthesis available to independent producers.

signification as strictly planned factors contributing to a representation of contents.

Transposed to the arena of the stage, the "live" performance of such compositions boils down to pressing ENTER on a computer keyboard and ends with the approximately ten minutes of silence required to rewire and equalize (EQ) equipment for the performance of the next track. Because of this, in academic computer music circles, the popular alternative to real-time computer playback is to play compositions previously recorded on digital audio tape (DAT), typically in a darkened auditorium with the audience facing an unused and blackened stage.[5] To avoid these uneventful tediums, many contemporary ambient producers' preferred approach to performance involves multichannel real-time tape manipulation—DJing—incorporating as many DAT drives, CD players, and turntables as can be arranged. Like direct computer playback, this method of performance allows for the "live" playback of digital sound files, plus it has the added advantages of allowing for real-time manual editing and mixing of a producer's

5 · This scenario is the audio equivalent to the white walls of the museum, in which an attempt is made to engage a "neutralization" of space so that "true art" may exist in-and-of itself, timeless and transcendent of cultural context. Of course, the cultural development of such "neutral" environments is a social (political) process, the frailty of which is reflected in the designing of such spaces so as to keep the "real world" out (darkened and silent auditoriums, white and windowless galleries, etc.). The elitism and discrimination behind such spaces was heavily critiqued by constructivists in the 1920s, whose arguments have been repeatedly updated since the 1970s by such groups as the Guerilla Art Action Group (GAAG), Artists Meeting for Cultural Change (AMCC), the Guerrilla Girls, and so on. While such critiques are rather widely accepted (or at least acknowledged) within the visual and performance arts, they are largely unknown to, and unrecognized by, musicians. The reason may lie in the manner in which contemporary industry-based music production and distribution emphasizes broad product placement and consumer accessibility, structured for consumers to "take the music with them" into cars, busses, homes, businesses, restaurants, and clubs. In this manner, the "neutralization" of space engaged by music is not locationally fixed but is rather a manifestation of the internalization of musical stylings (genres and artists) by consumers and producers as extensions of their subjective selves—a far more insidious and economically volatile relationship to deconstruct.

own input sources, as well as the intermixing of other producers' audio and external sound sources (an eschewing of authorship and establishment of referentiality). In terms of economies, such "live" performance becomes a representation of the productive processes of repetition. However, the deconstructive values I wish to infuse this multiplicitous economy with are currently (perhaps hopelessly) circumvented by popular musical codes around performance as a consumer process, through which the performer is required to exist as a celebrity (including personas of humility), and all sounds recorded and ambient are exalted only for their production of exchange value.

It is in this latter spectacular manner that the economic viability of DJ performance as an instrumental medium has been established, both within underground clubs and dominant culture (as exemplified by the global economic success of rap, house, and techno). And as the majority of contemporary ambient music events are organized by club promoters who deal with DJs on a regular basis, one would think that a stratification between DJing and "live" performance of conventional theatrical instruments would no longer exist. But this is not the case, particularly within the price scales of contemporary ambient performance. Speaking from personal experience, after hearing that my standard presentation techniques do not involve keyboards or other traditional theatrical instruments, I have had countless organizers reduce their initially proposed "live performance" fee by more than half. In New York, the common practice is to ask producers to DJ for free (with a "we're all trying to make this happen together" snuck into the invitation somewhere), regardless of the fact that people attending the events must pay a cover charge at the door to enter. Such prioritizations of performance strategies enter the realm of cultural production by presenting an economic boycott which effectively censors the efforts of post-spectacle, computer-based producers—restricting our access to the cultural outlets and economic means which both allow and rely upon studio production. The long-term effect of such an environment is contemporary ambient's restriction to popular musical paradigms of production and presentation.

The cultural impact of such restrictions can be traced in The Orb's rise to supergroup status. Fronted by Alex Paterson, a former A&R person for E.G. Records, which handled Brian Eno's original ambient releases, The Orb is largely credited for the mass popularization of contemporary ambient music. Like many contemporary ambient producers of the late 1980s and early 1990s, The Orb's early performances took the form of DJ sets in "chill rooms" which were secondary to main dance floors in nightclubs and raves. The decentralized placement of such performances seemed to be reiterated in the DJ's preference for anti-spectacle audio, including 1970s ambient music, sound effects, minimalist music, and musique concrète. Despite the notoriously transcendental overtones of rave "chill rooms," several producers (myself included) found affinities with the contemporary ambient movement through a realization that most of the stylings and circumstances of contemporary ambient performance invoke histories which emphasize a social (material) positioning of the audience in relation to the sounds being performed.

With time, there began to be entirely contemporary ambient events, including Ultra-red's opening of Public Space in Los Angeles in 1994. Ultra-red drew from their experiences as activists to present "ambient music in its most obvious, material manifestation: the sound culture of everyday life":

> From the start, we were not in the least persuaded by ambient music's pretensions for spirituality or its mystical capacity. Perhaps this cynicism stemmed from the very real experience of harm reduction and needle exchange. No amount of ecstasy—particularly spiritual ecstasy—completely erases the body and its material needs. In fact, the capacity to experience pleasure is directly linked to the quality of care given to the body. This we learned from harm reduction. The same seemed to apply to a musical movement which took its inspiration from a history of avant-garde music, from Russolo and Cage to Eno and The Orb. Central to that tradition was the notion of giving audition to the sound culture of the everyday: finding musical pleasure in the mundane soundscape.[6]

6 Ultra-red, "intro duction: noise and public space three years later," p. 1, http://manoafreeuniversity.org/projects/soundings/kompendium/pdfs/ur_introduction.pdf, last accessed January 14, 2021.

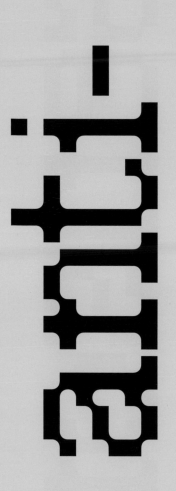

sensor

But in the absence of any large-scale understanding of how to stage events around a concept of decentralization, most organizers and producers grappled at the most familiar performance strategy associated with free-form and a-structural music: the neo-bohemian, progressive rock festival—a thoroughly mainstream marketing strategy which, by the early 1990s, was already consuming the rave community. In this manner, contemporary ambient producers fell prey to all of the demands of other stage and personality-based performance strategies. Decentralization was overwritten by a concept of authorship, and any remnants of desire among producers for anonymity only resulted in confusion. Disoriented producers took to darkened stages, beginning and ending their sets unannounced and intermixed with opening and closing DJs. Meanwhile, audiences now faced stage-forward, asking if the show had begun and complaining that they could not spot their favorite stars clearly on stage. By 1996, when The Orb took center stage at New York's Roseland Theater with drummers and guitarists on hand, dominant contemporary ambient performance was no more than a musical staging of "The Eighteenth Brumaire of Louis Bonaparte."[7] Frustrated and confused by the lack of populist satisfaction derived from such stagings, producers, organizers, and audiences declared "ambient is dead." Few seemed to realize that this disorientation was a by-product of the *functionality* of contemporary ambient production. Few seemed to realize that contemporary ambient's inapplicability to a prog-rock metaphor involved a disclosure of prog-rock and all music's site-specificity and non-universality, and suggested the development of new performance strategies.

---

7   The opening words to Karl Marx's "The Eighteenth Brumaire of Louis Bonaparte" (originally published in 1852 in *Die Revolution*, a German monthly magazine published in New York) are: "Hegel remarks somewhere that all the events and personalities of great importance in world history occur, as it were, twice. He forgot to add: the first time as tragedy, the second as farce." Available online https://www.marxists.org/archive/marx/works/1852/18th-brumaire/ last accessed January 14, 2021. In this instance, the tragedy of Eno's ambient was the treadmill tragedy of existential isolation and self-reduction. The farce of The Orb's ambient was the prog-rock packaging and staging of a premise claiming roots in anti-spectacle.

Under the collapse of prog-rock staging, a number of producers, including Oval, Scanner, Dumb Type, and myself, increasingly turned toward production methods that attempted to address processes of deconstruction present in our own methodologies. For many of us, digital editing and computer synthesis emerged as the primary studio process capable of representing a decentralization of authorship through the sampling and resynthesis of other peoples' recordings, as well as by exploiting a high-profile technophobia present in the popular media which identified computers and the Internet as threats to personal identity. In this manner, the subjectivity of the creative process, as well as the listening process, was audibly connected to a social history of inputs and cultural variables.

Despite this newfound enthusiasm among producers on a market level, the retreat from prog-rock aesthetics was accompanied by a new emphasis on the homogenizing power of quantized rhythms and an increasing resistance to a-structural and beatless performances. As for myself, proposals to incorporate texts with releases so as to familiarize listeners with my own rationale behind particular processes, as well as to generate discourse around materialist listening practices, were discouraged by the record company I was signed to, resulting in semiotically burdened and textless covers such as that of *Soil*.[8] Record labels began pressuring contemporary ambient producers to produce neo-urban music: trip-hop, abstract beats,

8   Terre Thaemlitz, *Soil* [CD album]. New York: Instinct Records, 1995.
    A viewing of the CD booklet is intended to mimic an emergent awareness
    of processes of social contextualization. The front of the CD booklet
    features a triangular excerpt of a photograph of trees, playing on popular
    contemporary ambient associations with nature as a transcendental
    signifier. The back of the booklet shows the entire photograph, with the
    triangular excerpt transformed into the inverted pink triangle, symbolic
    of Queer empowerment and the "Silence = Death" HIV/AIDS activist
    and education movements. The inside of the booklet contains a photograph
    of a used condom discarded in woodland soil, which would trigger a
    (hopefully recognizable) socially developed response in the listener, such
    as intrigue, beauty, offense, and/or disgust. The title *Soil* was not only
    a cynical stab at amnionic "Mother Earth" ambient music titles, but also
    a reference to the verb to ejaculate, indicative of the masturbatory
    nature of music production and creative processes (including those I my-
    self engage in). Similarly, the image of the condom references the phallo-
    centrism implicit to conventional definitions of such processes.

drum & bass, ambient jungle, and acid jazz. Both in sales and performance, this new predominance of rhythm serves to synchronize and pace a production's reception, using the restraints of simple mathematics to invoke a simplification of interpretive formulas. Only a few committed record labels that had developed steady followers continued to release a-structural contemporary ambient material, and they now found themselves flooded with submissions from producers rejected or abandoned by other labels. This frustrating situation was poignantly described by Ultra-red:

> Without financial support (however contingent as provided
> by the academy), no fair effort can be engendered. What is left?
> [...]. Becoming tied to the whims of marketplace innovation
> (the spectacular failings of avant-garde 'development') as witnessed in the current 'death of ambient' phenomenon? Yes,
> the market declares its death in the moment a cleavage appears
> between ambience metaphysicians and the sound materialists.
> Death? Or, reinvention. Quick, declare its death before it
> constitutes an audience around itself. Stigmatize the music,
> and by association, its audience. And accomplish this task
> at the precise moment art practices develop which actually
> intervene upon the conditions of reproduction.[9]

One intriguing result of the contemporary ambient record industry's transition toward neo-urban music is a renewed emphasis of the DJ as the ideal contemporary ambient performer. However, this return occurs in the most conventional of ways, engaging familiar images of DJs as the celebrities we have come to know through the rap industry and nightclub followings. There is no secondary displacement of identity, as was suggested (however unintentionally) by early "chill rooms." The DJ is center stage and fully reconcilable with dominant personality-driven performance structures. As a personality figure, the DJ's sense of individuality is used to generate authenticity, thus distracting one from questions of authorship (as opposed to encouraging a direct deconstruction of such issues).

---

9   Ultra-red, via correspondence in May 1996.

◆ c:\dokumente und einstellungen\ulf gurke\desktop\alle musik\andrea toms zwei\andrea toms 44,

◆ Datei   Bearbeiten   Struktur   Funktionen   Geräte   Optionen   Notation   Module   Fenster   Hilfe

| Solo | Raster Takt | Quant. | 32 | Part-Farben | 266. 1. 1.   0 | Marker ▼ | Edit.verbinden |

A M C T	Spur	Kanal							
	Audio 1	1+2	Kick Drum-4.wav						
	Audio 2	3+4	DPA Overhead 1-4.wav						
	Audio 3	5	10						
	Audio 4	6	10						
●	Audio 5	7	iphop.WAV						
	Audio 6	8	ik 4.2.wav						
	Audio 7	9	Audio 7						
	Audio 8	10	6						
	Spur 9	11	9						
	Spur 10	12	10						
	Spur 11	13	10						
	Spur 12	14	12						
	Spur 13	15+16	103.WAV						
	Spur 14	17	14						
	Spur 15	18	7						
	Spur 16	19	16						
●	Spur 17	20	7						
	Spur 18	21	Git1 C414#13.aif						
	Spur 19	22	Spur 19						
	Spur 20	23+24							
	Spur 21	25+26	Spur 21						
	Spur 22	27+28	Rausch cutups mix.wav						
	Spur 23	29							
	Spur 24	31+32	24						
	Spur 25	33							
	Spur 26	34	Spur 26						
	Spur 27	35	korg.WAV						
	Spur 28	36	Spur 28						
	Spur 29	37	Spur 29						
	Spur 30	38	Spur 30						
	Spur 31	39	Spur 31						
	Spur 32	40	Spur 32						
	Spur 33	41+42							

▶|

🏁 Start   ◆ c:\dokumente und ein...

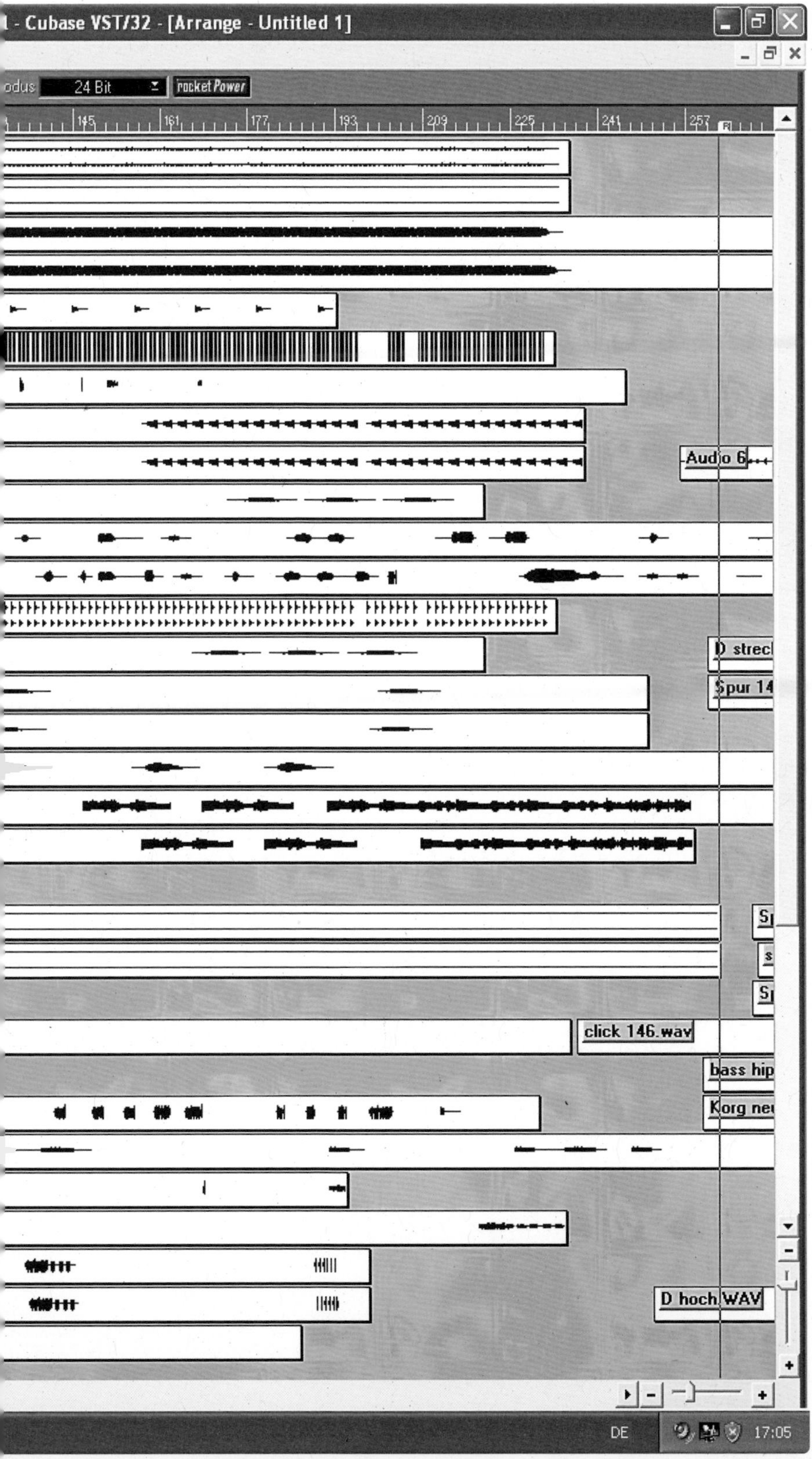

I - Cubase VST/32 - [Arrange - Untitled 1]

odus 24 Bit ▾ rocket Power

145 161 177 193 209 225 241 257

Audio 6

D strecl

Spur 14

Sp

s

Sp

click 146.wav

bass hip

Korg neu

D hoch WAV

DE 17:05

The listener's act of consumption no longer emphasizes the traditionally modernist fetishization of a producer's creative output. Rather, it
reflects a tertiary commodification of the DJ's selection and performance of other producers' outputs as the ultimate in informed commodity fetishism. In a cultural atmosphere which conflates the consumption of music with the definition of self, what process of
self-identification can a consumer more closely relate to than the very
act of consumption? Thus, the popular elevation of the DJ as celebrity
allows consumers to not only purchase music, but to vicariously
engage in the DJ's expert and near pathological process of consuming
music. Transferred to the realm of contemporary ambient performance, this condition is the essence of New York's illbient scene.

In the disaffecting aftermath of the death of ambient, illbient
has emerged to clarify electronica's reconcilability with institutions
of modernity, a jargon-infused attempt for dominant viability within
the crumbling necropolis.

In a classic affirmation of modernist hegemony, the illbient construction of content occurs within the sound itself in a theoretical sus-
pension of temporality and objecthood, suggesting "a full immersion
of sound and visual electrotectural experimentation in the temporery
[*sic*] autonomous."[10] Much like Pablo Picasso's colonialist appropria-
tion of African masks in *Les Demoiselles d'Avignon*, the illbient DJ
seeks to conceal processes of recontextualization through ideologies
of decontextualization and replacement, as "each and every source
sample is fragmented and bereft of prior meaning—kind of like a
future without a past. The samples are given meaning only when
re-presented in the assemblage of the mix."[11] The suggested decontextualization of inputs into a melting-pot mixology is used to declare
an open sense of community. However, its practical effect as a context
whose precise moment of production denies contextuality enacts a
process of social homogenization implicit with any humanism that
replaces an unresolvable collision of contexts (difference) with a

10 SoundLab (Beth Coleman and Howard Goldkrand), "Enter the Mix,"
    on the installation *Enter the Mix* at the Whitney Museum of American Art
    Biennial Exhibition, 1997.
11 Paul D. Miller (a.k.a. DJ Spooky That Subliminal Kid), "Flow My Blood
    the DJ Said" [song lyrics], in *Songs of a Dead Dreamer*. New York: Asphodel
    Records, 1996.

fictional reconciliation of contents (unity). For illbience, this replacement of difference with unity is necessary precisely because humanist ideology is unable to sustain concepts of irreconcilability which inhibit the cohesion of a singular and sharable human condition. It is this paradox which poses the greatest challenge to the mechanisms of illbient ideology.[12]

The illbient community's representation of modernist ideology is appreciatively reciprocated by art institutions, such as with the SoundLab event for the 1997 Whitney Biennial Exhibition. The event's placement within a gutted floor in a Wall Street building was not so much deconstructive as ironic. Impromptu sidewalk café tables were placed near the main coffee bar, invoking the high-modernist café atmosphere that museum officials have come to associate with progressive thinking. One might still overhear patrons debating Sartre, but in this café, the sound of improvisational jazz was replaced by the turntable instrumentalists and free-form poets of the illbient community. Abstract textural 35-mm slide projections and film loops permeated the space, as free-form dancers invoked the motions of 1960s performance. The proposed "aesthetic merger of the digital with the analog"[13] did not reflect the use of digital media (which was largely absent) as much as an ideological fissure of the antiquated with the recumbent. And, in typical fashion and without naming names, there are numerous stories of only partial or no compensation of expenses to performers at the event—a condition which I emphasize is not unique to SoundLab, but to contemporary ambient performance in general.

Despite the contention that "SoundLab happenings are urban illbient community actions, encouraging a dynamic, contentious cultural production rather than passive consumption,"[14] for both audience and performers, the primary communal relations of the Sound-Lab were precisely the capitalist relations of traditional Marxist commodity fetishism. By its own declaration, the SoundLab is a

12 Seeing as this is the very paradox which has been debated within the visual and performing arts for decades to little avail, I find it difficult to infuse this observation with a sense of urgency, threat, or immediate transformative potential.
13 Coleman and Goldkrand, "Enter the Mix."
14 Ibid.

manifestation of the social relations between the products of artistic production, emphasizing the alienation from labor which results in fetishism. Producers, along with audience members who "enter the mix," "build [their] own different [*sic*] engines, creating [...] personal vocabularies"[15] which function as metaphors for the labors of individuals acting separately. The sum of these difference engines being exchanged in the marketplace of the SoundLab results in the emergence of seemingly independent contents (illbience) which are mutually engaged by both audience members and performers. As a material exchange relationship, audience members exchange money to vicariously engage in the productive acts of performers—to consume (and hence reclaim) their daily relationship to experiential processes of observation by being transformed into their own mixing boards. Conversely, performers are encouraged to distance themselves from their individual labor so as to produce a communal illbience which shrouds processes of direct financial compensation in mystery.

The continuity between all of the aforementioned venues for contemporary ambient performance—DAT playback in darkened auditoriums, DJing in side rooms at raves, prog-rock staging, or immersive illbient events—is their failure to address the undesirable yet unavoidable implications of performance as a strategy of representation within the mechanisms of consumer capitalism. While such venues claim an avant-garde inhabitation of a cultural periphery, they fail to address the peripheral as a strategic fictional response to a mythology of the core. A fiction, which, when unaddressed, loses strategy and adopts the language of humanism until it poses no greater threat to social convention than an expressionist's scratchings upon a museum's walls. Similarly, contemporary ambient emerges from materialist traditions which have been dismantled by their inability to successfully strategize the paradoxical—from constructivism and musique concrète's claims to represent a utopian social(ist) consciousness, to minimalism's quest to isolate the production of contents in the individual's interpretive process while somehow having those contents be sharable. Thus, the crisis of post-spectacle "live" contemporary ambient performance arises from this historical inability to react to the limitations of performance methodologies as they function within the very core of relations which contemporary ambient asserts it is

15 Ibid.

positioned to critique. The economic viability of performance remains contingent upon abstract and homogenizing audience relations which inhibit the incorporation of fracturing diversity. The performance itself serves to represent a reconciliation of intent with process, tempering any attempts to elucidate the sustained collision of distinct and simultaneous economies of representation and repetition.

I am forced to accept the manners in which this circumstance conditions my own reception as well as production. My own objectives for performance are hopelessly diffused in their actualization. Every composition's abandonment of rhythm imparts an uninvited dissension from the incessant drums which accompany the march of cultural inertia, only to be resurrected through reappropriation by institutions of the avant-garde. Each attempt for clarification on my part contributes to an air of arrogance and self-distinction, which erodes my relationship to the cultural outlets I wish to nurture. I am compelled to tip the hat to the popular observation that "at least an Orb concert or illbient event can get people together." But then again, I remind myself, so does Sunday Mass, and the act of congregation can never be distilled from the politics of social organization.

All things considered, this is why I can't get paid to DJ a-structural audio.

April 1997

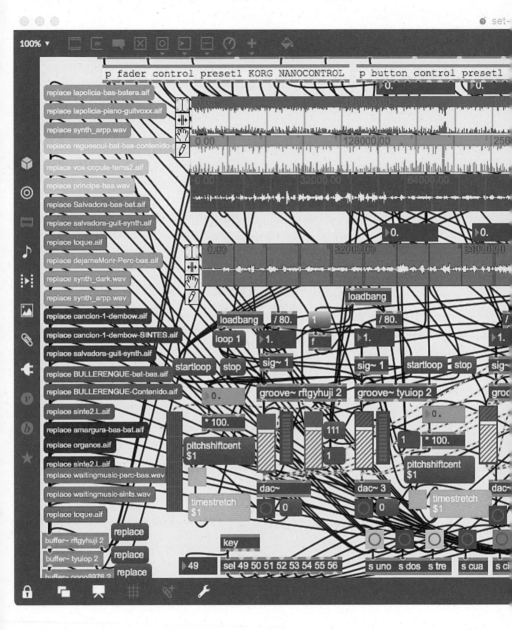

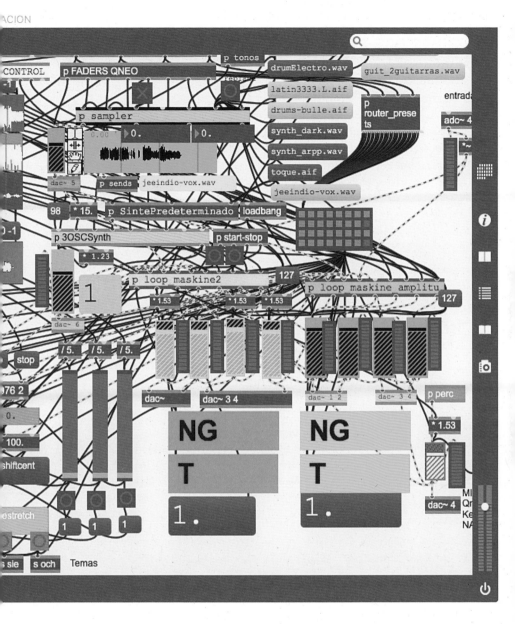

The TOPLAP Manifesto

TOPLAP stands for Transnational Organisation for the Permanence of Live AudioVisual Programming. TOPLAP has been collectively developing, exploring and promoting live coding since it was formed in a smoky bar in Hamburg in 2004.

Live coders expose and rewire the innards of software while it generates improvised music and/or visuals. All code manipulation is projected. Live coding works across musical genres, and has been seen in concert halls, late-night jazz bars, as well as "algoraves." It is inclusive and accessible to all.[1]

"Original" TOPLAP draft manifesto
(with focus on music performance)

We demand:

—Give us access to the performer's mind, to the whole human instrument.
—Obscurantism is dangerous. Show us your screens.
—Programs are instruments that can change themselves.
—The program is to be transcended—Artificial language is the way.
—Code should be seen as well as heard, underlying algorithms viewed as well as their visual outcome.
—Live coding is not about tools. Algorithms are thoughts. Chainsaws are tools. That's why algorithms are sometimes harder to notice than chainsaws.

---

1   Source: https://toplap.org/wiki/ManifestoDraft. Reprinted by kind permission of TOPLAP. For more, see https: //toplap.org/about/, https://toplap.org/wiki/Main_Page, last accessed April 10, 2021.

We recognize continuums of interaction and profundity, but prefer:

- —Insight into algorithms
- —The skillful extemporization of algorithm as an expressive/ impressive display of mental dexterity
- —No backup (minidisc, DVD, safety net computer)

We acknowledge that:

- —It is not necessary for a lay audience to understand the code to appreciate it, much as it is not necessary to know how to play guitar in order to appreciate watching a guitar performance.
- —Live coding may be accompanied by an impressive display of manual dexterity and the glorification of the typing interface.
- —Performance involves continuums of interaction, covering perhaps the scope of controls with respect to the parameter space of the artwork, or gestural content, particularly directness of expressive detail. Whilst the traditional haptic rate timing deviations of expressivity in instrumental music are not approximated in code, why repeat the past? No doubt the writing of code and expression of thought will develop its own nuances and customs.

Performances and events closely meeting these Manifesto conditions may apply for TOPLAP approval and seal.

It's Incredibly Nerve-Wrecking To Be On Stage and Not Gesture

Recording under the name Dane Law, and teaching and researching music and sound design, Adam Parkinson has built a practice across the nexus of tools, electronic musicianship, algorithmic composition, and performance with machines. Working at modular gear maker Rebel Tech, he even once delved into a generative music box created by pioneering composer Raymond Scott—which he says has informed his own ideas about modular contraptions, triggering patterns, and rhythms. So Parkinson is a perfect sounding board for exploring the relationship between the seen and unseen, human improvisation, and machine rules in performance.

Peter Kirn: Let's start with your music. *Algorithmic Music for Synthesised Strings* sounds through-composed, but also organic. Are we hearing the single outcome of a particular code or heuristic, or what is the process that leads to the outcome?

Adam Parkinson: I see what I'm doing as improvising with algorithms. What you hear on that album is a modular software performance system, which offloads certain decisions to algorithmic processes—mostly simple trigger processors or Markov chains [a probabilistic model for sequences of events] alongside oscillators, randomizers, and so on. Sometimes I'll just press "start" and sit back; sometimes I'll be more hands-on and tweak parameters in real time.

I normally record everything in a single take. I'll often generate huge amounts of recordings, and then pick out the best three-to-five-minute sections. Most Dane Law albums are culled from hours of such improvisations.

I'll sometimes import the audio and add a few extra layers of ambience through spectral freezing [audio effects] and so on, and on rare occasions I'll do a bit of editing to layer or stitch things together. But I really, really hate editing. Once I start editing, I don't know when to stop, and get sucked into a quest for impossible perfection.

I'm glad it sounds organic. I love computer music that sounds totally digital and organic and free and improvised at the same time, things like Fennesz's album *Venice* and Jim O'Rourke's *I'm Happy and I'm Singing*. Both are about twenty years old now, but they really shaped the way I think about sound.

PK: Actually, backing up to that point—what does "algorithm" mean to you? Is there something new to computer algorithms that makes them fundamentally different than other rule-based music? Otherwise, is it essentially related to processes like *kotekan* (interlocking pattern techniques) in Balinese *gamelan* music or contrapuntal and voice-leading principles?

AP: I often wonder about this—I feel "algorithm" is used to describe such a range of processes that are often very different in kind. The algorithms I use are all relatively simple rules or probability models that produce interesting results musically (to me at least).

Here, I've always been interested in Alex McLean's work [a researcher, and developer of pattern-based live coding music environment TidalCycles]. He opened my eyes to what feels like a lengthy tradition of algorithms that I think would include *kotekan* and other things like change ringing of church bells. I think there's a degree to which Western music theory is a bunch of algorithms, and you can code simple principles and rules to generate diatonic chord sequences and so on.

Then, I think a lot of the emerging and vital critical discourse around algorithms is generally referring to the sort of data mining and machine learning-related stuff that Google, Facebook, and others are doing. This isn't a toolset or a discourse I ever address in my own music, though it obviously has huge implications for our lives in the future. I think Holly Herndon's work is a good example of music that's exploring some of those issues and ideas.

PK: I wonder how you feel about live performance and what's visible. If we compare it to the live coding scene, the primary means of interaction is typing—though some people do plug in extra controllers and whatnot. What does it mean to remove the gestural interaction from the performance? Is that live composing, in a sense, or should we think of the coding itself as being like a gesture?

AP: Even though I don't live code myself too much, my exposure to the scene really shaped my approach to live performance. I loved the idea that live coding was exploring the unique affordances of the computer for making music, rather than trying to turn the computer into a gestural instrument modeled on instruments of the past.

For a while, I thought gestural interaction and the pursuit of it just got in the way of electronic music. It seemed like a truism that "laptop sets are boring" and that the performers could just be checking their e-mail or filing their tax return. I often thought electronic musicians ruined performances with gestural interaction, making their music too busy or always changing things—there's a feeling you get that you should be doing something when you're on stage, even if the music doesn't require it.

I was inspired by people like Mark Fell, and his resistance to gesture and movement, and some of the reductionist / lower case improvisers, people like Radu Malfatti who are prepared to **stand on a stage and do very, very little** for quite a long time. It's **incredibly nerve-wracking to be on stage and not gesture, but that approach always appealed to me**, even if I've never quite **gone there myself.**

I also remember seeing Autechre around 2005, on the tour supporting *Untilted*—for me, that was when their music became super-gestural feeling and organic, sounding really free and improvised, and they performed in total darkness, so you had no idea what they were doing. I think I decided then that gesture was a red herring and that we were just trying to fit this new, exciting form of music into what had gone in the past.

All this said, I think there are many people doing interesting gestural things with computers, and my own anti-gesture rhetoric has probably mellowed. I love Atau Tanaka's performances with cardiac (ECG) and brain (EEG) sensors, and Laetitia Sonami's instruments [e.g. the "Lady's Glove" sensor-filled handwear used for gestural interfaces].

freeze

Mickey-Mousing

PK: That's how you approach those interfaces—but since you're also teaching, I'm curious how you communicate those performance interactions to students. And those students must vary a lot in their own backgrounds and experiences, right?

AP: The students I teach come from a whole range of different musical backgrounds and have different amounts of musical and performance experience.

Ultimately, I try to get them to think about the computer as a musical instrument, whatever it is they're interested in and whatever their musical background, and get them to explore the unique affordances (yep, that term again) that it offers. People quickly develop their own workflows and unique ways of using software—something like Ableton Live offers so many different ways of approaching music and performance.

It's exciting to see the ways of working that people end up developing. We've been doing live-streamed concerts in lockdown, and I've seen all sorts coming from the students—from analogue acid techno in someone's kitchen, to interactive digital audiovisual pieces.

More people understand that musicality means so many different things now, such a broad range of skills, and much of what I do when teaching is just trying to introduce people to different possibilities for expressing themselves musically, encourage them to run with it.

PK: Right—and I know you've dealt with that in a range of tools, from modular environments to Pro Tools. So how does that human-machine combination work?

Any composer sees their ideas change once in the hands of musicians—either by the players giving you feedback, or in their interpretation of the score. What is that relationship like with the computer? Is it fair to call this a collaboration—even when the machine doesn't have agency in the way a human being does?

AP: I like to see my music as something that emerges from encounters between technologies, sounds, and myself. I think "collaboration" could be one way of understanding or representing that encounter. For me, making music is never about being

able effortlessly to impose or execute some musical idea—the process of executing always shapes and changes that idea. I've found that Bruno Latour's Actor–Network Theory and the once-fashionable object-oriented philosophy provide useful tools for thinking some of this through.

PK: To put it another way, is there also a collaboration with the humans behind that technology?

AP: Whilst it's certainly a collaboration with these instrument builders, engineers, and so on, I think music making also involves countless examples of technologies being used beyond the intentions of the designers and having a life of their own. The most cited example of course is the Roland 303 [bass synthesizer] and acid house, but everything from guitar feedback in rock and roll to close-miked crooners are stories of technologies being put into networks that reveal hidden affordances that weren't intentionally designed into them.

PK: That gets to the point of what is designed into them, too, though. Do computer-based musical environments encode compositional ideas and conception in a way that's unique? I suppose a fretboard or the setup of an autoharp or tuning of a gong all have their own encoded compositional ideas, but, on the other hand, you wouldn't really confuse them with a score. Is a computer environment able to encode more of those compositional structures?

AP: That's a good point—Thor Magnusson has done some really good work on this (I'm thinking of his "Epistemic Tools" article for *Organised Sound*) as has Robert Strachan in his book *Sonic Technologies* (and no doubt others). All these computer-based musical environments and DAWs we use suggest that certain ways of making music are more natural than others—diatonic music, 4/4 beats, and so on. And by allowing you to do certain things, they make you feel like you *should* do those things—like editing all the mistakes out of a performance in Pro Tools. They're all embedded with certain ideologies about music making.

I don't know if it's more or less than acoustic instruments. I suppose I see them all on a continuum. On acoustic instruments, we see people using "extended techniques" to move beyond constraints—bowing the gong like Eddie Prévost or laying down the guitar and letting it go out of tune like Keith Rowe. What would be the equivalent of this sort of structure-breaking behavior with Ableton Live, I wonder?

I think that all the music programming languages we have access to nowadays give people really open environments to work within, where there aren't too many rules encoded, although there's probably a set of cultural pressures and expectations shaping what people think their music should sound like.

I'd say that a beautiful example of going beyond the ideas encoded in the software is Hans Koch's *bandoneonbook*—a laptop running a [custom-built Cycling '74] Max patch, which modulates the feedback between the mic and the speakers when it's closed—his taking advantage of a certain design quirk, allowing him to play it like an accordion, opening and shutting the MacBook and holding the keys.

PK: That's a great way to approach how to present the computer as an instrument. You know, I always wanted to write a send-up of the infamous Milton Babbitt essay "Who Cares if You Listen?" (even if he reportedly hated that title). It'd be "Who Cares if You Watch?" But to what extent does it matter that a performance gesture be visible? It seems heavily contextual. How have you tackled this as a researcher—or in your own music?

AP: I wrote a conference paper a few years back with Ollie Bown and Renick Bell where we tried to get people to guess what laptop performers were doing based on listening to a recording—but not seeing the performance. We had a theory that listeners didn't need to see the gestures to know what performers were doing. We didn't prove anything, of course, but the people who took part turned out to be quite good at identifying "live" elements, as well as spotting certain pieces of software and idiomatic approaches to liveness.

In my view, with an awful lot of what you see at a "traditional" classical concert, for instance, the gesture is expressive rather than actually triggering sound. You can't see the fingers of a concert pianist, but there's a degree of trust, and you know that pianos are terrible for checking e-mail.

There's a bit in Mark Katz's *The Phonograph Effect* where he talks about how with the advent of recording, violinists started adding more vibrato to their playing to compensate for the lack of expressive visual gesture. Performers' gestures can be expressive and an essential part of the performance even if they aren't affecting the sound, it's part of the way in which they embody and express the music they're creating.

Joining the Dots—
Sketching the Outlines of a Floating Girl

君に伝えたいことが	All the things I want to tell you
君に届けたいことが	All the things I want to give you
たくさんの点は線になって	Countless dots start to form lines
遠く彼方へと響く	Echoing to the faraway distance

livetune, "Tell Your World," 2012

Much has been made of the differing reactions of Japanese audiences and those of the rest of the world to Hatsune Miku, the teal-haired sixteen-year-old who burst onto the scene as a mascot for the new Vocaloid software series in 2007, and then to her first live concert two years later in 2009. It is said that those who had been following her since her emergence—adult men and women, but mostly men—cried when she took to the stage. Today in 2021, those who became her followers and welled up and were captivated by her spectacle, as well as those who scorned and touted the end of humanity in opposition, have matured fourteen years. Exponential growth in technology has meant that chip sizes have diminished while our iPhones have undergone countless mutations. And yet, she remains much the same. Her longevity could also be attributed to the fact that she straddles so many different aspects of speculation that it almost creates a sense of human likeness. With her various iterations and global fame, even inspiring the dead back to life (2.0Pac, Michael Jackson), what significance does this shift toward the virtual have on the future of musical performance?

    I feel it is important to lay out the cultural groundwork that may have led to the different level of acceptance of the "Vocalo" movement in Japan. For instance, one of the most obvious points is the ubiquitous tradition of reading pictures: manga and the world of fandom, conventions, cosplay, etc., as well as the prominence of on-screen cartoon characters with exaggerated voices. With regard to animation, the voice becomes a key element in the completion of the illusion. Known in Japan as 2.5D culture, voice artistry is celebrated, and voice actors are elevated to stardom themselves, sometimes even performing on stage with their character counterparts. Between the two-dimensional animations and the three-dimensional voice actor, the illusion of a real existence can be concretely attributed to the addition of the acted voice. As a side note, although animated content is increasingly gaining popularity outside Japan—Netflix is currently investing heavily in Japanese animated content—"Western" voice acting feels much closer to how real people sound, whereas Japanese voice acting, and I would add standard acting as well here, has always looked and sounded like "an act." This "bad acting" has always been a point of contention, where Japanese acting—for instance in drama series where exaggeration is inherent—has been viewed critically, at least in terms of the quality of the acting. In contrast, animation dubbing has always remained questionable, with non-Japanese audiences preferring the original voices to the dubbed.

This leads us to the second point. Western culture has always insisted on "authenticity" in performance, whereas this is not necessarily so in Japan, where illusion is just as readily accepted. In any case, the popular music industry is so carefully and meticulously controlled, constructed, and dehumanized that the shift to an actual illusion could be seen as logical. Acts like the Gorillaz are virtual characters, but the four are all based on the real members of the band. They are perhaps closer to their extensions, and they are routinely shown on stage, albeit behind a veil, together with their animated counterparts.

As with most other cultural movements, the acceptance of Miku was down to a multilayered and complex accumulation of vectors bubbling under the surface which eventually broke through and affected what followed, rather than being down to a singular cause. In this essay, we look at the context within which the Hatsune Miku phenomenon took hold—particularly in Japan where technological advances are put to use without much angst; think of robotics and the care industry—and the possible cultural locations where she could be rooted.

仮想（ヴァーチャル）と現実の狭間で	Between the cracks of dreams and reality
私は生まれ　愛されてきた	I was born and loved
今だけ　お願い　夢をみさせて	Let me dream just for now

KazuP, "Innocence," 2007

Hatsune Miku (whose name means "first sound of the future" in Japanese) is a virtual idol: the third and most successful in a series of animated pop stars developed using the Yamaha Vocaloid engine. She was launched in 2007 by Crypton Future Media under a creative commons license. Subsequently adopted by a vast community of online users, Hatsune Miku has become a kind of mirror, revealing to each new user their own desires.

She is not the first virtual idol to have ever been created, but none have enjoyed as much success or attention as her. The virtual idol has predecessors; for instance, Rei Toei in *Idoru*,[1] the cyberpunk trilogy by William Gibson, or Date Kyoko (pronounced Daté), the first Japanese computer-generated idol created by the talent agency Horipuro. The former is a fictive social commentary on the technologized, feminized, Japanese (at least by name) other, while the latter is precisely the object of that commentary. Combining the best computer graphics technology available at the time with the voice of an unnamed artist, Horipuro created in Kyoko a character with cropped hair and a crop top and cast her in music videos. While the distinctly 1990s aesthetics of their creation would appeal to today's obsession with retro, only a handful of fan sites still contain traces of Kyoko. It would be an interesting feat to trace what is left of this forgotten star. Another example is Ann Lee: In 1999, French artists Philippe Parreno and Pierre Huyghe bought the copyright to a Japanese manga character and lent the image to various artists including Liam Gillick and Dominique Gonzalez-Foerster. In their project with Ann Lee, titled "No Ghost Just a Shell"—in a nod to the animation film by Mamoru Oshii—they explore and exploit the image of a nondescript side character who most probably would never have been used anyway. In 2002, they signed over the rights to her image to the character Ann

---

1   *Idoru* is the second book in William Gibson's science fiction "Bridge" trilogy: William Gibson, *Idoru*. New York: Viking, 1996.

Lee herself, signaling the end to both the project and her existence. This illustrates how, if virtual entities aim to supersede the lifespan of a real-life idol, no attempt has yet come near to achieving this longevity.

It is probably fair to say that in all cases they have been products of the male gaze. However, one could argue, which *real* idol is free of such a claim? Of course, there are male characters in the Vocaloid series, just as there are male idols in real life, but they do not compare to their female counterparts in terms of revenue. As the documentary *Tokyo Idols* (2017) by Kyoko Miyake shows, the huge *aidoru* (idol) market is largely supported by older men, some of whom have given up their jobs to become full-time fan-club members. These men seem harmless and genuinely interested in the success of their chosen idol, some describing the girls as if they were their own daughters. They are being sold their own dreams, and these dreams are, or seem to be at least, very much attainable, not least because there are said to be more than 10,000 self-professed idols in Japan. They are deliberately marketed so that they seem just within reach, so that they are not cosmetically worked on as their K-pop counterparts famously are. Their attention is also equally shared out among each of the fan-club members who line up after their shows to shake their hand and to chat in a truly socially egalitarian manner. The manager stands with a timer and lets the fans know when their time is up, rotating them around. Perhaps it is this remarkable sense of equality in the community that they are attracted to, as well as the fact that fans are almost guaranteed to receive what they paid for in becoming members, even if this means a measly one-minute conversation with their favorite idol under the careful watch of officials[2]—a very transactional approach that renders the idols replaceable with a few algorithms. This carefully constructed idol industry is surely one of the reasons for the ease with which Crypton Future Media decided to make the jump from illustrations to full-blown stage performances in the first place.

---

2   Kyoko Miyake, *Tokyo Idols* [documentary film]. Tokyo et al.: A Brakeless / EyeSteelFilm production for WDR, ARTE, Superchannel, BBC, IKON, DR, SVT, and NRK, 2017.

Vocaloids were initially developed to eliminate the need for backing singers in recording sessions, thus cutting time and production costs. Due to increasing numbers of home-studio producers, the ratio of singers to producers was becoming problematic. Vocaloid was seen as a long-overdue development in terms of electronic music synthesis, as almost every other known instrument had already been synthesized decades ago. Drum machines and synthesizers had become integral to the music production process, and while vocal effects such as the vocoder or its predecessor (Bell Labs' "Voder") did exist, the industry had been unsuccessful in producing a voice synthesizer. The Vocaloid, however, gave producers total digital control over melody, timbre, and even emotion.

Early trials used the voice of a professional singer, but this was deemed somewhat lacking, and a voice actor named Saki Fujita was chosen specifically for the "Lolita-like" quality of her voice. Subsequently, the voices of well-known J-pop singers have also been recorded, packaged, and sold: Gackt, a popular Japanese musician, became the Vocaloid "Gackupoid," and Megumi Nakajima's voice became "Megupoid." Currently, there are more than a hundred official Vocaloids. Other software—such as UTAU, a free vocal synthesis engine that allows a user to essentially become their own Vocaloid—have since been developed too.

Aside from being her voice, Miku is also the creative commons-licensed image of Hatsune Miku. Her visual aspect is predictably where she receives the most coverage, as it is perhaps more striking and complex. There are a few rules that apply to her visual image according to her creators: Her hair is of an iconic teal blue, which corresponds to the teal tone of the buttons of the Yamaha DX series of synthesizers, a version of which she sports on her sleeve in the very first official image drawn of her by artist Kei Garou (a.k.a. KEI) for Crypton Future Media, the Japanese sound and media company to which Miku officially belongs. She is also 158 centimeters tall and weighs a measly 42 kilograms, and she will never grow older than sixteen years of age. What differentiates her from most other animated characters is her creative commons licensing: CC-BY-NC, also known as Creative Commons or Attribution-NonCommercial, the official umbrella term her licensing would fall under, which means that as long as the original copyright holders are credited and, crucially, this image is not created for the purpose of commercial business, anybody

has the right to recreate her image and redistribute it, dependent on a few provisos. For example, rules on her distribution include not debasing her image with sexual or violent content and not using her image for political purposes. Giving this freedom to her fans has largely been the secret to her success, with platforms such as Deviant-Art or BowlRoll or Niconico (the Japanese equivalent to YouTube) serving as natural proliferation platforms.

そう 僕は 君が望むピエロだ	Yes, I'm a pierrot you want
君が思うままに 操ってよ	Just manipulate me as you want

40mP, "Karakuri Piero" (Clockwork Clown), 2011

There is no definitive linear-historical sociocultural timeline that led to her success. Instead, there are various dots that can be joined and multiple linearities that can be suggested. She is hard to pin down, but it is this elusiveness which I find particularly intriguing. Of course, one very clear line is that humanity has been looking for ways to animate the inanimate for thousands of years; the first known puppet, for example, can be traced back to Egypt around 3,000 years ago. Failed attempts at resurrecting the dead and fembots gone wrong in the past have never hindered the human desire to create animate beings and play God. More specifically to Japan, it has been suggested that the traditional Japanese puppetry of Bunraku could be a useful lens through which we can begin to unravel the idol phenomenon, though this would be looking mainly at her stage performances.[3] Bunraku as an art form dates back to the sixteenth century and, in contrast to Nō and Kabuki theater which are also recognized as UNESCO Cultural Heritages, Bunraku involves the use of puppets. These are operated by three puppeteers who are dressed in black on stage to signify their invisibility. The other component is a duo made up of the *tayu* (the chanter responsible for the narration of the story as well as the individual characters) and the shamisen player (the musician who creates

3   Louise Jackson and Mike Dines, "Vocaloids and the Japanese Virtual Vocal Performance," in Sheila Whiteley and Shara Rambarran (eds), *The Oxford Handbook of Music and Virtuality*. Oxford: Oxford University Press, 2016, pp. 101-10.

the atmosphere in perfect harmony with the chanter). The fact that these elements are laid bare for the audience to see, and yet they feel drawn into the illusion even more, is something that intrigued Roland Barthes as well as Susan Sontag.[4]

While it is true that, in a general overarching timeline, some similarities can be drawn and the dots can be joined between Miku and Bunraku, it is also the case that these traditional Japanese forms of theater are no longer popular, especially among regular young people in Japan, and they are increasingly seen as reserved for a special upper class. More and more, we find that traditional craft, ceremonies, and techniques are dying, with few people having the patience to learn these lifelong trades. In most cases today, they are propped up by foreign interest and governmental support. This makes it less probable that those who brought Hatsune Miku to the stage in 2009 had the direct and conscious intention of incorporating the techniques of Bunraku into her performances. Nonetheless, there are more vectors to explore, which may act as missing links between the art of traditional Japanese puppetry and the Vocaloid concert.

It is no secret that the Japanese consume much of their information and entertainment through the reading of figurative drawings. Reading manga and watching animations are daily routines for many, and their content varies according to which audience they are geared toward. For children, they are categorized and divided by gender: *Shōnen* manga (boys) and *Shōjo* manga (girls). These are dated categorizations, however, and are now, from both the consumers' point of view as well as those of the authors, on the brink of becoming redundant. Adult manga is often associated with pornographic material, especially the content that is known outside Japan, but there are a host of other genres such as thrillers and mysteries, crime stories, fantasy dramas, as well as the more mundane.

Animation, as a logical extension of the manga category, in fact exists in synergy with it, as well as with a third component: the fans. Perhaps comparable to the *Verfilmung* (adaptation to film) of novels, the animation of manga is often debated in terms of whether the final product is true to the original or not, resulting in the reproduction of

4   See Roland Barthes, "On Bunraku," *The Drama Review*, vol. 15, no. 2: Theatre in Asia (1971), pp. 76–80; and Susan Sontag, "A Note on Bunraku," *The Threepenny Review*, no. 16 (Winter 1984), p. 16.

the same manga or parts of it, or even complete readaptations by other animation studios. As the word animation itself suggests, it brings movement and therefore a time element into the discussion, breathing new life into the characters. But most important, I would say, is the addition of another dimension, namely the voice.

The voice, as an entity that floats somewhere between the depicted figure and the bodily source, acts as a gelling agent for the character and, if chosen well, can become their defining characteristic. Voices in much (and especially in Japanese) animation act out a distinct, exaggerated tone and delivery, perhaps overcompensating for the more limited detail of drawn faces; after all, less emotional information can be gleaned from a cartoon facial expression in comparison to the subtleties in that of a living face. Due to this—and to the additional fact that female voice actors often play both genders, including young boys, due to their malleable vocal range (in an ironic twist to the Kabuki and Nō period where women were not deemed skilled enough to play women)—voice acting necessitates much skill and artistry. This may be one of the reasons for the elevated position of voice artists in Japan. The floating voice between the two-dimensional and the three-dimensional attaches itself to the character and gives off the illusion that it is helping it to move along, smoothing out the lines, and ironing out any jagged edges. Interestingly, the revealing of the source of the actual voice does not take away from the effect it has on the illusion of the character. Mladen Dolar uses the example of the Wizard in *The Wizard of Oz* to illustrate that the voice separated from the body has an omnipotent power, but as soon as the body to which it belongs is revealed, the magic disappears.[5] The Wizard tells Dorothy, "Pay no attention to that man behind the curtain!" (The man being himself, the owner of the booming voice known as the Wizard, afraid of being found out.) In contrast, the male and female voice actors in Japan, especially Vocaloids, enjoy a celebrity status that almost rivals the success of the characters themselves. This could be seen as part of the long tradition of acknowledging the artistry involved in the creation of illusions, traceable back to the voice artists that accompanied the traditional Japanese theaters of Kabuki, Nō, and Bunraku.

5   Mladen Dolar, *A Voice and Nothing More*. Cambridge, MA: MIT Press, 2006.

everyday

In a further visual sense, the origins of manga are said to be found in Kabuki and Nō theaters. Many scholars have pointed to the link between Kabuki and manga, whereby frequently manga is visibly informed by Kabuki.[6] On the one hand, there are educational manga books that explain the different traditional theater forms, and on the other, more interestingly, visual links can be made between the positioning of the figure in dramatic moments in a manga cel and the trained, dramatic Kabuki actor's pose, for example.

Nō theater also brings parallels, being known for its masks on which a range of expression can be subtly realized by the use of light, shadow, and slight angles. The masks have been compared to the faces depicted in manga, the biggest difference being the size of the eyes. Nō masks only have small eyeholes through which the actor must communicate various expressions, which in turn the viewer must catch and read. I will not delve into the history of the large, sparkly, Westernized manga eyes within the scope of this essay, but there is an expression in Japanese that may be suitable here: When a person is described as being expressionless or has the look of someone whose mind is wandering off, it is described as their "eyes turn to dots." The mouth on a Nō mask is also very small, and the *shite* or leading actor narrates and performs the character's voice from behind it, requiring the viewer to create the connections between character and voice. There is a definitive link to be made here with the construction of the talking figure in animation, where the movement of the lips and the voice are never quite synched, and there is no deliberate attempt to make it look as though they are. Again, it is asked of the audience to "fill in the blank" as it were. What becomes important is the viewers' subconscious (or conscious) choice to buy into, or rather eek out with the help of props, the illusion they want to see, while knowing full well that it is one, and being shown explicitly that it is one.

It is also worth noting that the idea of feminine beauty around this period was based on the modest glimpse of smooth pale skin in the dark. This is laid out beautifully in Jun'ichirō Tanizaki's *In Praise*

---

6   Junko Kuwako, "The Origins of Cool Japan: Considering Dramatic Communication," *Journal of Bunkyo Gakuin University, Department of Foreign Languages and Bunkyo Gakuin College*, vol. 9 (2009), pp. 250–55.

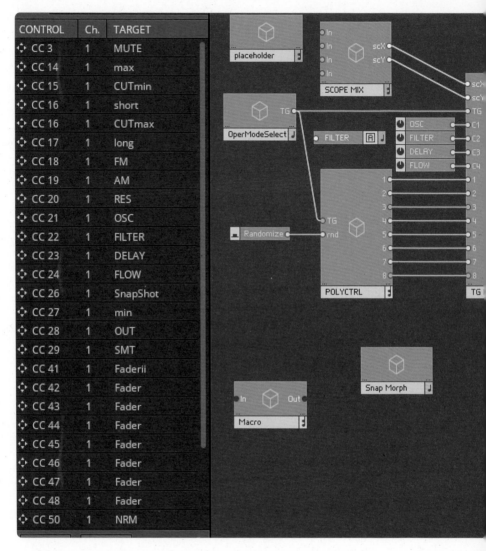

CONTROL	Ch.	TARGET
✦ CC 3	1	MUTE
✦ CC 14	1	max
✦ CC 15	1	CUTmin
✦ CC 16	1	short
✦ CC 16	1	CUTmax
✦ CC 17	1	long
✦ CC 18	1	FM
✦ CC 19	1	AM
✦ CC 20	1	RES
✦ CC 21	1	OSC
✦ CC 22	1	FILTER
✦ CC 23	1	DELAY
✦ CC 24	1	FLOW
✦ CC 26	1	SnapShot
✦ CC 27	1	min
✦ CC 28	1	OUT
✦ CC 29	1	SMT
✦ CC 41	1	Faderii
✦ CC 42	1	Fader
✦ CC 43	1	Fader
✦ CC 44	1	Fader
✦ CC 45	1	Fader
✦ CC 46	1	Fader
✦ CC 47	1	Fader
✦ CC 48	1	Fader
✦ CC 50	1	NRM

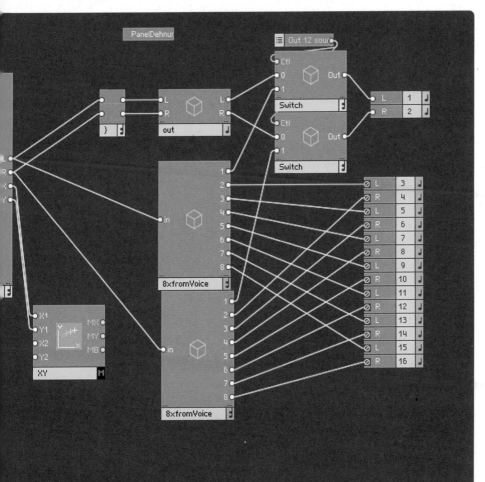

of Shadows.[7] Teeth were blackened with coal in order to not distract from the glow of the porcelain skin. The less on show, the more beauty can be presupposed. In the pre-light bulb period when only the scant light from candles was used, the beautiful silk kimono with golden embroidery, or the lick of red and black lacquered bowls were shown in their best light. Hatsune Miku's visibility too is conditional on darkness. Her image is completely dependent on the light waves and particles catching on a treated screen, or else she slips away.

For now, Miku's "liveness" must remain imagined. Though her core fans do not seem to need any help with this—new technologies will keep her updated and looking fresh until, eventually, she may even break through the final frontier of the screen, allowing her the freedom of the whole length of the stage. With developments in artificial intelligence, she may even achieve full autonomy, preprogrammed with obligatory celebrity tantrums. Although exclusive to Japan, I think music journalist Tomonori Shiba was right when he described the Hatsune Miku phenomenon as riding "the third wave of the Summer of Love."[8] The first wave was Woodstock, California, amidst protests against the Vietnam War in the 1960s; the second was the UK rave scene of the late 1980s and 1990s, protesting against Thatcherism. Shiba claims that the utopian ideals of sharing and distributing works around the networked fandom, and the infectious euphoria surrounding Hatsune Miku in online communities—fighting against the depression of the music industries' tightening grip on copyrights and property around the advent of the Internet and streaming—constitutes the third wave. There is a kind of inclusiveness or togetherness gained through a communal feeling of being at the cusp of something revolutionary, whether it be love, drugs, or online creation, a concept of sharing that is inherent to musical experience.

Finally, I would emphasize the importance of a different aspect of hers that has not yet been mentioned: her ever-growing catalogue of derivations. If left to the fans' own devices, there is a danger that all the baggage that comes with the female body, its soft curves and

7   谷崎潤一郎, 陰翳礼讃: Jun'ichirō Tanizaki, *In Praise of Shadows* [1933], trans. Thomas Harper and Edward Seidensticker. Sedgewick, ME: Leete's Island Books, 1977.

8   Shiba Tomonori, *Why Hatsune Miku Changed the World*. Tokyo: Ohta Publishing, 2014, p. 54 (author's translation).

viscous membranes, all of this is in danger of being completely wiped off the grid in favor of a slick, techy ideal:

> As long as we cannot yet completely migrate out of our bodies and transcend into the ether of ones and noughts, there is an urgent need to reflect these unwanted yet beautiful materialities in our virtual spaces. Hatsune Miku's strength lies in her fluidity of form and her ability to mutate according to her fans. The capitalist father and the company to which she belongs is always looking for ways to keep growing, and she has found a wider, global audience also in the West, multiplying and diversifying as she grows. However, if this phenomenon is to be useful at all, she must subvert the gender/race norm narrative of a Japanese female virtual assistant, incorporating versions such as pregnant Miku, throwing up Miku, menstruating Miku, sweaty Miku, etc., embracing all the physical bodily blubber much like the way the original cyberfeminists of the 1990s set out to do.[9]

The current trend towards "virtual" social-media users could be a site where this vision is actualized, with the CGI-generated influencers becoming beacons of this nature. Popular virtual Instagrammers such as Imma, Meme, Liam Nikuro in Japan, and Lil Miquela, Shudu, and Kernel Sanders, who are more globally recognized, have the potential to chip away at the taboos of virtual existence, thereby doing the same for our living existence.

---

9   Mari Matsutoya, "Queering Miku: Cyberfeminism and the Art of Queering a Virtual Pop Star," in Michael Ahlers et al. (eds), *Musik & Empowerment*. Wiesbaden: Springer VS, 2020, pp. 115–32, here p. 131.

Looking at Music as Movement

1. Looking at Dance

Dance is a spectacle—music we can look at. At the same time, dance is always a subjective bodily experience. First, there is the experience of the dancing person, who may be facing an audience, a dance partner, or a camera. Moreover, something about the spectacle of dance affects the people watching it. Within couple dance scene circles, there is a division between the two main groups of dancers: those who rely upon visual effects and those who communicate through bodily experience. Theoretically, concepts such as mirror neurons, prosthetic memory, or vibes[1] are used to grasp such mediations through dance. Regardless of whether they occur vis-à-vis a dancing crowd or via media representations on the cinema screen—visual impressions of body movements stimulate us physically. Looking at other bodies viscerally triggers something in our watching body. If we conceive of dance as *looking at music*, then this viewing pleasure also leads us to *feeling the music*, or rather to *feeling connected with other bodies through music*.

Hundreds of visual representations on rock testify to dancing people in Africa, India, Australia, Italy, Turkey, Israel, Iran, and Egypt all the way back to the Stone Age.[2] Even before they started to write or become sedentary, people danced together. Dance was so important to them that they captured it in images. Throughout the ages, representations of dance have framed our view of dancers through the dance settings they depicted ranging from ballrooms to colonial plantations. With the arrival of photography, postcards popularized the North American cakewalk in Europe and along the coast of West Africa.[3] Dance movies—especially those where people train for a final

---

1   Maria A.G. Witek, "Feeling at One: Socio-Affective Distribution, Vibe, and Dance-Music Consciousness," in Ruth Herbert et al. (eds), *Music and Consciousness 2: Worlds, Practices, Modalites*. Oxford: Oxford University Press, 2019, pp. 93–112.

2   Barbara Ehrenreich, *Dancing in the Streets: A History of Collective Joy*. New York: Metropolitan Books, 2006.

3   Astrid Kusser, *Körper in Schieflage: Tanzen Im Strudel Des Black Atlantic Um 1900*. Bielefeld: transcript, 2013.

performance—create communities of viewers who often become active dancers themselves.[4] Thus, *Beat Street* sparked the breakdance movement in the GDR. Television shows like *American Bandstand* popularized the twist, choreographies have been established in video clips for decades, dance competition shows run on all TV channels, and Jamaican dancehall-queen competition documentaries circulate on DVD all over the world, so that the newly crowned queens soon came not only from Jamaica but also from Japan or Canada. In 2019, Chance the Rapper sparked a public debate about selling dance moves on the online game platform Fortnite. Leaving aside the copyright debate and the unpaid child labor on TikTok, Snapchat, and other such media outlets—the company Epic Games knows what nerve it seeks to strike when it sells dance moves as so-called *emotes*. Looking at dance is touching and mobilizing.

In 2020, while everyone had to maintain social distance and just hang in there, the Angolan dance troupe Os Fenomenos do Semba catapulted the South African house track *Jerusalema* by Master KG (feat. singer Nomcebo Zikode) into the international charts. In the fall of 2020, *Jerusalema* became the most searched for song on Shazam. Thanks to the #Jerusalemadancechallenge, the Kenyan Parliament, female lawyers of the Cape Town High Court in high heels and robes, or a Zimbabwean youth organization social distancing and wearing face coverings immortalized themselves on YouTube and TikTok. They were followed by Italian nuns and Romanian firefighters, and finally by staff in European hospitals. The group choreography they performed derives from the Angolan dança da família ("family dance"). This in turn is based on a South African adaptation of the electric slide, which Jamaican Marcia Griffith popularized in 1983 with her video clip *Electric Boogie*. The Jerusalema dance challenge thus brought a prosumer practice to the workforces in German supermarkets and police stations that had been common to African dance music styles like kuduro since the early 2000s.

---

4   Melissa Blanco Borelli (ed.), *The Oxford Handbook of Dance and the Popular Screen*. London and New York: Oxford University Press, 2014.

2. Kuduro—Digitally Native within a Strong Dance Tradition

Kuduro ("hard ass") is electronic dance music from Angola, notable for its crass acrobatic dance moves. Kuduro happens in schoolyards, at children's birthday parties, in backyards, nightclubs, street corners, and minibus cabs, as well as for cell phones, social media, and shared hosting platforms. Kuduro is both hyperlocal and globally connected. In around 2005, many young Angolans started filming kuduro dance with their cell phones, sharing the videos from one phone to another via Bluetooth. Professional dance groups such as Os Muchachos de Tony Amado, Costuleta e Amigos, and Salsicha e Vaca Louca were quick to release dance instructions on DVD. Cell phones with built-in camcorders also then became ubiquitous in Angola.[5] Footage of kuduro dancers like Tictac and Cobra G circulated on cell phones, inspiring kids and teens to engage in dance battles on street corners.[6] Through such direct contact, the kids learned kuduro moves, later capturing them as visual artifacts in mobile videos. This meant they could document and disseminate their own dance practice with little post-production intervention or even censorship.

Kuduro's percussive computer-produced beats of around 140 BPM and belligerent, boastful lyrics are closely intertwined with so-called *toques*, expressive dance moves with meaningful names. As a general rule, if a dance move is picked up by a broad audience and danced at private functions, in schoolyards and discotheques, the kuduro song becomes a hit. Kuduro performers therefore strive to make their *toques* easy and enjoyable to perform. From around 2000, kuduro became the main youth culture in Angola and the Angolan diaspora, and in 2009 the national TV station TPA2 started broadcasting a weekly kuduro show called *Sempre a subir* ("Always on the up and up").

Former Michael Jackson impersonator and dancer Tony Amado brought kuduro to public attention in a television appearance. Initially designating only a single *toque*, kuduro came to denote a vast

5 Stefanie Alisch, "Angolan Kuduro: Carga, Aesthetic Duelling, and Pleasure Politics Performed Through Music and Dance," PhD diss., Universität Bayreuth, 2017.
6 Celestino Agosto Bali, a.k.a. BM (2012): Interview with Stefanie Alisch, For Os Kuduristas Campaign, Luanda, August 2, 2012.

complex of music-dance practices. Virtually every new kuduro song is released with its own dance step. The names of these *toques* usually refer to everyday events in Luanda. The piece *Engraxador* ("Shoe-shiner") by the group Os Namayer, for example, is dedicated to the many young shoeshiners in the dusty capital. The corresponding *toque* imitates the typical circular hand movement they use to polish shoes. Mauro Alemão's *Catolotolo* dance, with its convulsive twitches, was popular in 2014, when the joint-spasm-inducing chikungunya fever (locally known as *catolotolo*) was rampant. Kuduro combines knowledge of sound, lyrics, dance movements, and everyday events. More or less veiled sexual meanings often cannot be understood from the lyrics alone and are only revealed when the corresponding dance step is seen or actively performed. While dancing to the superhit *Apaga Fogo* ("Put out the fire," Noite Dia, 2011), for example, people wave their hands between their legs as if the crotch needed cooling, but paradoxically also as if they were fanning a fire.

As digitally native as kuduro is, it feeds on urban music and dance forms that have played a central role in Luanda throughout the twentieth century. Following independence in 1975, the vibrant live music scene collapsed. And since it is difficult to dance to socialist anthems, young people in Luanda listened to zouk from the Antilles and Cape Verdean music scenes during the 1980s and early 1990s.[7] They danced trendy dances like bruxo e bruxa, brotuto, bungula, kabetula, kapreko, or vaiola. In the early 1990s, house and Eurodance filled the discotheques of Luanda, and Angolan artists such as Beto Max, M.G.M Zangado, Eduardo Paim, and Bruno de Castro produced their own electronic dance music. By this time, young people in Luanda had already formulated a popular dance vocabulary, which they practiced and developed along with the new kuduro beats. The practice of *dance calling* carries itself from the Angolan quadrilha off-shoot rebita from the beginning of the twentieth century through to kuduro. The person who calls out the dancers' names and dance moves over the microphone is called an *animador*. Because they give clear instructions, kuduro dancers can highly focus and thus move

---

7   Marissa J. Moorman, *Intonations: A Social History of Music and Nation in Luanda, Angola, from 1945 to Recent Times*. New African Histories series. Athens and Ohio, IL: Ohio University Press, 2008.

excellently and transgressively.[8] As in other DJ cultures, the absence of live musicians opened up a space for prominent dance performances on stage and on the dance floor. Kuduro dance draws from Luanda's dance traditions such as rebita, semba, carnival dance, and kizomba, but also from breakdance videos and martial arts movies. Kuduristas also like to be inspired by the choreographies of Congolese dance bands like Koffi Olumidé, Werra Son, or Fally Ipupa.

Kuduro dance frequently features a move I have called "Switching over."[9] This entails taking a particular position with shoulders drawn up, arms tucked in, back arched, buttocks stuck out. After a short pause, dancers maintain this cramped pose when they resume movement. This is different from a break or freeze in breakdance or jazz dance, where the break position completes a move or resolves into it. "Switching over" typically occurs some time into a kuduro solo dance performance by expert dancers. It seems as if the performers work themselves into a state to accumulate enough charge to "switchover" when they reach a point of criticality.

Kuduro is one of many Black Atlantic dances where the break, the pause, is full of tension. In jazz dance, cakewalk, house dancing, tango, breakdancing, and, surprisingly, the polka, the break is crucial in a flow of movements. According to Robert Farris Thompson, the break in the polka enabled Afro-Argentinian dancers to relate their Congolese kinetic repertoire to a European one.[10] As such, the break became the moment of connection for them. The break is a moment of historical connection between dance styles from different periods, but it is also an intersection in another sense: it is the moment of posing for a mirror, an audience, or a camera.

The moment of "switching over" can be understood as a residue of the photographic pose that remains in the dance. This freeze

---

8   Stefanie Alisch, Lecture: "Towards an Epistemology of Sound Systems," 6th Global Reggae Conference—Reggae Innovation and Sound System Culture II, University of the West Indies Reggae Studies Unit, Institute of Caribbean Studies, Kingston, Jamaica (February 13-16), February 14, 2019.

9   Stefanie Alisch, "Switching Over: Reflections on the Intersection of Dance and Visual Media in Angolan Kuduro," in Ute Fendler, et al. (eds), *Revolution 3.0: Iconographies of Radical Change*. Munich: Akademische Verlagsgemeinschaft, 2019, pp. 329-60.

10 Kusser, *Körper in Schieflage*, p. 92.

marks a change of quality in the performance, a break between planned choreography and playfully transgressive improvisation, a performative surplus. "Switching over" allows kuduro performers to make eye contact with the audience and the camera during a series of fast moves, and thereby to return the gaze, to affirm their presence.

Stage delivery, camera usage, and audience interaction are highly intertwined in kuduro. Kuduristas typically perform into cameras, sometimes using intense facial expressions and gesticulations. The *cara feia* ("ugly face"), typical of kuduro, consists of bizarre facial contortions mimed directly into the camera. Camera operators find it hard to capture kuduristas without an intense camera-orientated delivery, which is called "camera grilling" in media parlance. Visibility is an important resource in Angola and in kuduro, as attention can facilitate social advancement. Almost every kuduro act performs with dancers, and featured female singers like Noite Dia, Titica, or Fofando are often excellent dancers themselves. It is paradoxical: Kuduro dancers provide the most blatant eye-catchers on stage and yet only the other performers know their names; their working conditions are highly precarious, and every performance exposes their bodies—their working tools—to intense risks. Many kuduristas therefore start their career as dancers and, in time, advance to the status of singers.

3. Airness—the Metaloop of Looking at Music

Body movements can create sound. Some ethnomusicologists conceive of instrument playing as patterns of movement. Dance responds to sound, as in DJ performances, for instance, but dancers also shape a certain sound event with their movements, for example, at djembe festivals in Mali.[11] Since 1996, the Air Guitar World Championships have been playing with the fact that sound production can be triggered, underscored, dramatized, or counteracted by body movements. Like in a bar or disco, contestants on stage play air guitar to rock songs by better-known or less well-known musicians. According

---

11 Rainer Polak, "Performing Audience: On the Social Constitution of Focused Interaction at Celebrations in Mali," *Anthropos: International Review of Anthropology and Linguistics*, vol. 102, no. 1 (2007), pp. 3–18.

to Sydney Hutchinson, "air guitar on stage is a performance art that plays with that expression of masculinity, that uses it as material, exposes it, makes it strange, and exaggerates it."[12] The ethnomusicologist shows that successful air guitarists translate musical knowledge into body movements. Their role models are not only guitarists, but also increasingly other air guitarists. For the jury, the decisive criterion in the competition is not the perfectly synchronized choreography, but airness—an elusive performative quality, a serious persiflage that makes embodied rock expertise visible.

In the early 2000s, while some comments sections were still mocking DJs working away at unplugged mixing decks with bombastic gestures on afternoon TV shows, others were already organizing the first air DJ championships, as part of open-air festivals, for instance. A popular video documents the air DJing performance of an anonymous man reaching peak form.[13] With a distorted face and a sweaty curl glued to his forehead, he goes wild, plucking, playing air keyboard, shaking his shoulders, undulating and jerking his body, as if his instrument were an electric fence rather than a plastic folding chair. This air-DJ show grants an energetic surplus and an almost intolerable tension to a semi-exciting dance track. By illustrating the sound events with detailed body movements—I call this *kinetic Mickey-Mousing*[14]—the air DJ tells us about his own rave experience. With a mixture of irony and seriousness, he provides us with knowledge about the sound that is playing, teaching us how to feel it. The 2005 Australian air DJ champion Gandalf Archer instructs a dance class in key DJ moves like hand-on-ear-and-head-to-side (pre-listening), rotate-hand-to-the-left (rewind record), pump-finger/fist-in-air (freak out) at a dance school. The 2017 #AusAirDJ champion Electric Postman does not even add a track to his video. Providing the beat are the engine noises of a tractor, attached to which Electric Postman lets loose on a small lifting

12 Sydney Hutchinson, "Putting Some Air on Their Chests: Masculinity and Movement in Competitive Air Guitar," *The World of Music* (new series), vol. 3, no. 2: Music, Movement, and Masculinity (2014), pp. 79–103.

13 See "Air DJ Contest" [video], YouTube (posted November 18, 2019) https://www.youtube.com/watch?v=9WyjV2HHFW4 accessed April 9, 2021.

14 In movie parlance, Mickey Mousing refers to the detailed accompaniment of all plot events with music.

platform. The meta-joke: The jolting tractor not only provides sound and motion impulses but also references the DJ software of the same name.

Back in Angola, a video shows small children playing "DJ set" in a backyard. In front of them, the two boys of around four years old have precisely arranged toy DJ equipment on a surface—paper laptops, white cables, and electronic waste. Around it, they perform gestures like pre-listening on air headphones, applying effects, and increasing and decreasing the volume.[15] They also have an intern and a fan who support them from the side. Using mouth-percussion, the two young air DJs even deliver their own techno sound. They thus embody not only techno's movement patterns, but also its sound production. Other air DJs mix on ironing boards amidst tall grass, among seaweed on the ocean floor, at a workbench with a circular saw, or they play with equipment they have drawn in the fresh snow with only a few hand movements.

These airy performances afford a looking at music that takes the performative intertwining of sound production and body movement ad absurdum. The production of overdriven electric guitar sounds does not require physical labor that supposedly only men can perform, rather, the electric amplification of sound constitutes masculinity through rock music. The notion that the performance should be loud enough to fill a club or stadium and thereby determine how other people feel and act, is where gender becomes effective. In rock, the amplification of sound creates a dynamic relationship with bodily expression. The sound gets louder and more distorted, gestures grow ever larger, so that at the end the hyperbolic buildup needs to dissolve into spinning on the floor or the smashing of guitars. Playing air guitar and air DJing are to popular music what drag is to gender. The playfully hyperbolic performance lacks a material basis. By convincing the audience, despite the obvious blank, air DJs or guitarists demonstrate that any connection between sound and body movement perceived as natural is ultimately produced through performance.

15 See "Mano A Mano Produções" [video], Facebook (posted October 18, 2018) https://www.facebook.com/manoamano.producoes/ videos/1915749138505609/ accessed April 9, 2021.

Kinetic Mickey-Mousing is, however, not the only way to fill the void created by the decoupling of body movement and sound production. Since the early 2000s, female or non-binary live acts such as Heidi Mortenson, Kevin Blechdom, and Planningtorock have combined their own music with performance art. These elaborate performances tend to distract from the equipment or sound production even though they are of paramount importance to the overall effect of these acts. It is noteworthy that these artists also explore gender issues. The stage performance of sound artist Farahnaz Hatam, on the other hand, consists of her sitting on a chair in front of her computer, hands in her lap, while the code she has written runs through digital sound synthesis in SuperCollider, generating sounds. Why do women have to take on this additional labor or ostentatiously refuse to do it? What are the privileges that encourage a person to make a sound their own, to incorporate sounds?

In recent years, mobile video has become the ubiquitous medium. Since the early 2000s, I have been observing how, from BMX riding to kizomba couple dancing, prosumer-produced video clips or professional productions are received via computer or phone screens. The influence of the digital revolution has rather intensified these bodily practices, increasing their relevance instead of making them disappear—as feared in the early days of the Internet. Thus, the reception of body movements via mobile video reconfigures our relationship to popular dance. The possibility of pausing, rewinding, slowing down, or infinitely replaying the mediatized movement sequence and comparing our own version with the execution of others leads to a detailed globalized reception and, as a consequence, to increasingly virtuosic and, at the same time, increasingly standardized bodily practices. For example, for several years now, participants at dance festivals have via mobile video immortalized previously highly individual movement sequences of certain dance teachers. These videos circulate among adepts who internalize the signature style of dance teacher couples. If we wish to grasp popular dance as *Looking at Music*, we must not fall prey to certain figures of thought, even when presented to us by dancers and dance teachers who mobilize national identity as a resource, as do some journalists: we must be wary of exceptionalism (Angola has the greatest dancers!), essentializing notions (Africans have rhythm in their blood, Europeans dance poorly because they have no relationship to their bodies), and

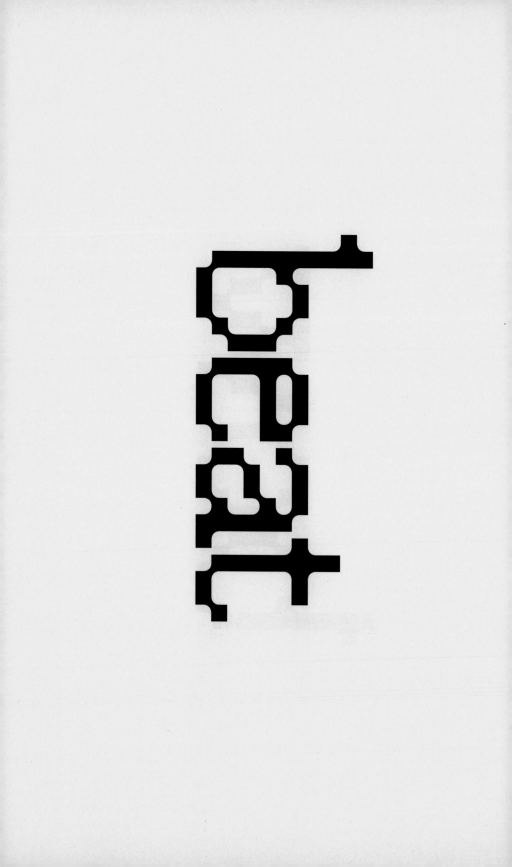

techno-determinism (digital music practice automatically puts dance at the center).

Music affects us as a multimodal experience. Sound, body movement, and lyrical content refer to each other, guide our attention, and, as a total package, present us with dense narrative, affective, and aesthetic affordances. Sound studies have already deconstructed visual primacy. Perhaps we can now speculate about kinetic primacy.

Translated from the German by Kevin Kennedy

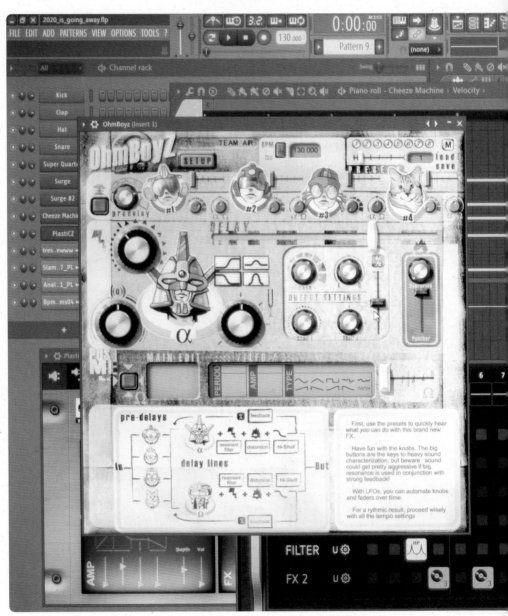

Program: FL Studio, Version 11, ca. 2013

01:02:03:13.66
57 4 4 1
8 1 1
83 4 1
Quick Help
Region: 21 selected
Track: BD 2
Icon:
Channel: Audio 22
Freeze Mode: Pre Fader
Q-Reference:
Flex Mode: Off
Setting
Setting
EQ
Input 5
Channel EQ
Audio FX
Bus 1
Stereo Out
Group
Group
Read
Read
+19
-2,8
-1,1
Bnce
M S
M S
BD 2
Stereo Out
Edit
Functions
View
S
25
29
2 BD 2
3 BD 1
4 reverse
5 click
6 click1
7 Snare
8 sna...hall
9 sna...all1
10 sna...all2
11 tamb
12 tamb B
13 tamb
14 tamb C
15 shaker1
16 shaker2
17 shaker3
18 Vocals
30 Hohner
31 B52
Beats all#04.44
Beats all#01.8
Beats all#02.8
Beats all#03.8
Beats all#07.45
snare hall#02.20
sha
shaker
shaker#02.12
Re
Reality i
Reality is Gone_1_
shaker#08.8
itled_
Untitled_3#02 me
Untitled_2#01.1

10,6000   4/4   No In   CPU
115   /16   No Out   HD   1234 >>

↖ ∨   ✂ ∨   Snap: Smart ◇   Drag: No Overlap ◇

|33 |37 |41 |45 |49 |53 |57

Beats all#04.21   Beats al   Beats all#04.10 ○   Beats all#04.11 ○   ● Be

Beats all#01.21   Beats   Beats all#01.10 ○   Beats all#01.11 ○   Be

● Beats all#   ● Beats all#0   Beats all#02.10 ○   Beats all   Bea   Be   Beats   ● Beats a

Beats all#03.58 ○   Beats all#03.65   B   Beat   ● Beats a

Bea   Be   Beats al   Beats

● Beats all#07   ● Beats a   Beats all#07.10 ○   Beats all#   Beats all#07.41   ● Beats a

snare hall#02.24 ○   s   snare hall#02.32 ○   ● snare h

sna   snare hal   snare

sna   snare hal   snare

_7#01 m   Un   Untitled_7#01 merged.3 ○   Untitled_7#01

Untitled_7#01 merged.10   Unti

ged.4   shaker#03 merged.7 ○   shaker#03 merged.8 ○

shaker#03 merged.6 ○

● shaker#02.3 ○   shaker#02.21 ○   ● shaker#02.26 ○   shaker#1

Gone_1   ●   ● Reality is Gone_1_25#02   Reality is Gone_1_25#02.51 ○   ● Reality is Gone_1_25#02.   ● Real   shaker#1

● shaker#15.1 ○   shaker#15.3 ○

Vocals   Vocals   Vo   Vocals   Vocals

Untitled_3#02 merged.79 ○   Reality is   U   Reality   ● Untitled   ● Untitled_3#02 mer   Untitle

● Untitled_2#01.25 ○   ● Untitled_2#01.8 ○   ● Untitled_2#01.9 ○   ● Untitle

+ Lina Brion is advisor to the program officer of the Akademie der Künste, Berlin. Until September 2020, she was project coordinator in the Department of Music and Performing Arts at Haus der Kulturen der Welt, where she curated discourse programs for the music festivals, among other things. Brion studied cultural studies and philosophy in Berlin and Paris. She is co-editor (with Detlef Diederichsen) of *100 Jahre Copyright* (100 Years of Copyright, 2019) in the series *Bibliothek 100 Gegenwart* (100 Years of Now Library, 2015–19).

+ Detlef Diederichsen has been head of the Department of Music and Performing Arts at Haus der Kulturen der Welt since 2006, where he has initiated several series and festivals, including *Wassermusik*; *On Music*; and *Worldtronics*, as well as theme days, such as "Unmenschliche Musik" (Unhuman Music); *Doofe Musik* (Stupid Music); *No! Music*; and *100 Jahre Copyright* (100 Years of Copyright, 2019). He previously worked as a musician, music producer, critic, journalist, editor, and translator. Since 1980, he has released several records with his band Die Zimmermänner, most recently the album *Ein Hund namens Arbeit*.

+   Stefanie Alisch acts as chair for Theory and History of Popular Music at the Humboldt-Universität zu Berlin. There and at the Universidade Federal da Bahia in Salvador da Bahia she studied musicology, Portuguese and English. Parallel to her studies she was active as a DJ, gave radio and DJ workshops and worked in the Berlin music (technology) industry, for example at Native Instruments, Ableton or Jazzanova. Since 2009 she has been a lecturer and received invitations for project consulting, moderations, scientific, and journalistic publications as well as teaching assignments.

+   Peter Kirn is a composer working with electronic media, and a voice for expressive creative technology. His music spans experimental and club sounds, live performance, DJing, and work with choreographers and spatial media. At the City University of New York, he studied composition with Tania León and co-founded the Graduate Center's Contemporary Music Ensemble. He produces the daily music and live visual site CDM (cdm. link), is co-creator of the MeeBlip hardware synthesizer line, and has collaborated with TED, European Space Agency, ARTYPICAL, Sonar+D, Mutek, Gamma, Factory Berlin, Parsons School for Design | The New School, and others, as well as hosting Music-Makers Hacklab with CTM Festival.

+   Currently residing in Berlin, Mari Matsutoya's work reflects on the mediation between cultures, languages, and existing social structures, often playing with stereotypes, and focusing on the fissures and glitches that occur in their translations. Her focus is on language both as a mirror of reality and as a speech act—learned systems that sit on the fence directly between the visual and the sonic. Previous shows and performances include those at the Barbican Centre, London, Arndt Gallery in Berlin, Tokyo Wonder Site, and transmediale/CTM festival, Berlin.

+ Adam Parkinson is an electronic musician and sound designer and Senior Lecturer for Music and Sound Design at the London South Bank University (LSBU) School of Arts and Creative Industries / Creative Technologies. As Dane Law, he makes electronic music which has been released on Quantum Natives, Opal Tapes, and Conditional.

+ Terre Thaemlitz is an award-winning multimedia producer, writer, public speaker, educator, audio remixer, DJ, and owner of the record label Comatonse Recordings. Her work combines a critical look at identity politics with an analysis of the socio-economics of commercial media production. He has released over fifteen solo albums, as well as numerous singles and video works; her writings on music and culture have been published internationally. As a speaker and educator on issues of non-essentialist Transgenderism and Queerness, Thaemlitz has participated in panel discussions throughout Europe and Japan. He has lived in Japan since January 2001.

+ TOPLAP stands for the Transnational Organisation for the Permanence of Live AudioVisual Programming. TOPLAP has been collectively developing, exploring, and promoting live coding since it was formed in a smoky bar in Hamburg in 2004.

Das Neue Alphabet (The New Alphabet) is a publication series by HKW (Haus der Kulturen der Welt).

The series is part of the HKW project *Das Neue Alphabet* (2019–2022), supported by the Federal Government Commissioner for Culture and the Media due to a ruling of the German Bundestag.

Series Editors: Detlef Diederichsen, Anselm Franke, Katrin Klingan, Daniel Neugebauer, Bernd Scherer
Project Management: Philipp Albers
Managing Editor: Martin Hager
Copy-Editing: Mandi Gomez, Hannah Sarid de Mowbray
Design Concept: Olaf Nicolai with Malin Gewinner, Hannes Drißner

Vol. 8: *Looking at Music*
Editors: Lina Brion, Detlef Diederichsen
Coordination: Lina Brion
Contributors: Stefanie Alisch, Peter Kirn, Mari Matsutoya, Adam Parkinson, Terre Thaemlitz, TOPLAP
Translations: Kevin Kennedy
Graphic Design: Malin Gewinner, Hannes Drißner, Markus Dreßen
Type-Setting: Hannes Drißner
DNA-Lettering (Cover): Philipp Lehr
Fonts: FK Raster (Florian Karsten), Suisse BP Int'l (Ian Party), Lyon Text (Kai Bernau)
Image Editing: Scancolor Reprostudio GmbH, Leipzig
Printing and Binding: Gutenberg Beuys Feindruckerei GmbH, Langenhagen

The editors would like to thank all the artists who sent them screenshots for free use.

Published by:
Spector Books
Harkortstr. 10
01407 Leipzig
www.spectorbooks.com

© 2021 the editors, authors, artists, Spector Books

Distribution:
Germany, Austria: GVA Gemeinsame Verlagsauslieferung
	Göttingen GmbH & Co. KG, www.gva-verlage.de
Switzerland: AVA Verlagsauslieferung AG, www.ava.ch
France, Belgium: Interart Paris, www.interart.fr
UK: Central Books Ltd, www.centralbooks.com
USA, Canada, Central and South America, Africa:
	ARTBOOK | D.A.P. www.artbook.com
Japan: twelvebooks, www.twelve-books.com
South Korea: The Book Society, www.thebooksociety.org
Australia, New Zealand: Perimeter Distribution,
	www.perimeterdistribution.com

Haus der Kulturen der Welt
John-Foster-Dulles-Allee 10
D-10557 Berlin
www.hkw.de

Haus der Kulturen der Welt

Haus der Kulturen der Welt is a business division of Kultur-
veranstaltungen des Bundes in Berlin GmbH (KBB).

Director: Bernd Scherer
Managing Director: Charlotte Sieben
Chairwoman of the Supervisory Board: Federal
	Government Commissioner for Culture and the Media
	Prof. Monika Grütters MdB

Colophon

Haus der Kulturen der Welt is supported by

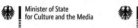

Minister of State
for Culture and the Media

Federal Foreign Office

First Edition
Printed in Germany
ISBN: 978-3-95905-492-8

Recently published:
Vol. 1: *The New Alphabet*
Vol. 2: *Listen to Lists!*
Vol. 3: *Counter_Readings of the Body*
Vol. 4: *Echo*
Vol. 5: *Skin and Code*
Vol. 6: *Carrier Bag Fiction*
Vol. 7: *Making*
Vol. 8: *Looking at Music*

Forthcoming:
Vol. 9: *A Kind of World War* (July 2021)
Vol. 10: *Re_Visioning Bodies* (August 2021)
Vol. 11: *What Is Life?* (September 2021)

Vol. 9:   *A Kind of World War*
Eds./Text: Anselm Franke, Erhard Schüttpelz
ISBN: 978-3-95905-494-2
            July 2021

Aby Warburg's famous lecture on the Hopi snake ritual in Arizona is one of the most commented art history transcripts of the 20th century. But while Warburg's essay is firmly anchored in the canon of art history, to a wider public—especially in Europe— little is known about its source, the snake ritual and its history. *A Kind of World War* is dedicated to what Aby Warburg largely ignored himself: that not only the ritual, but also the images of the ritual—to whose global distribution Warburg contributed— have a political history. The volume seeks to demonstrate that Warburg's art history, insofar it outlines an internal history of the European psyche, must be read in conjunction with its external counterpart, the history of colonization, war and cultural entanglement.

Vol. 10:   *Re_Visioning Bodies*
Editor: Daniel Neugebauer
Contrib.: Maaike Bleeker, Ayşe Güleç, Carmen Mörsch,
           Eliza Steinbock
ISBN: 978-3-95905-496-6
           August 2021

This volume plunges into a number of different archives and resurfaces with physical techniques: Eliza Steinbock finds love in the Lili Elbe Archive, Europe's largest collection of trans* and queer history; Carmen Mörsch describes how bodies that act as a medium for artistic expression communicate more than just art, inviting us to take a discrimination-wary view; Ayşe Güleç opens up an archive of migrant melancholia and speculates on stories that have ended in failure due to systemic racism. Maaike Bleeker slips into the role of Neo in *The Matrix* and plugs a data-transfer cable into our spinal cord to ask how intellectual knowledge and physical knowing condition one another.

Vol. 11:   *What Is Life?*
Editors: Stefan Helmreich, Natasha Myers, Sophia Roosth,
             and Michael Rossi in associatian with Katrin Klingan
             and Nick Houde
Contrib.:   Stefan Helmreich, Natasha Myers, Sophia Roosth,
             Michael Rossi
ISBN: 978-3-95905-498-0
             September 2021

"What is life?" is a question that has haunted the life sciences
since Gottfried Treviranus and Jean-Baptiste Lamarck inde-
pendently coined the word "biology" in 1802. The query has
titled scores of articles and books, with Erwin Schrödinger's
in 1944 and Lynn Margulis & Dorion Sagan's in 1995 being only
the most prominent ones. In this book, the editors curate and
speculate upon a collection of first pages of publications from
1829–2020 containing "What Is Life?" in their titles. Replies
to the question—and, by extension, the object of biology—have
transformed since its first enunciation, from "the sum of the
functions that resist death" to "a bioinformation system" to
"edible, lovable, lethal." Interleaved are frame-shifting interrup-
tions reflecting on how the question has been posed, answered,
and may yet be unasked.